I0011930

The Small Business' Guide to Social CRM

Build customer relationships that will accelerate your business

Craig M. Jamieson

Impackt Publishing

We Mean Business

The Small Business' Guide to Social CRM

Copyright © 2014 Impackt Publishing

All rights reserved. No part of this book may be reproduced, stored in a retrieval system, or transmitted in any form or by any means, without the prior written permission of the publisher, except in the case of brief quotations embedded in critical articles or reviews.

Every effort has been made in the preparation of this book to ensure the accuracy of the information presented. However, the information contained in this book is sold without warranty, either express or implied. Neither the author nor Impackt Publishing, and its dealers and distributors will be held liable for any damages caused or alleged to be caused directly or indirectly by this book.

Impackt Publishing has endeavored to provide trademark information about all of the companies and products mentioned in this book by the appropriate use of capitals. However, Impackt Publishing cannot guarantee the accuracy of this information.

First published: September 2014

Production reference: 1250914

Published by Impackt Publishing Ltd.
Livery Place
35 Livery Street
Birmingham B3 2PB, UK.

ISBN 978-1-78300-120-0

www.Impacktpub.com

Credits

Author

Craig M. Jamieson

Reviewers

Pramod Kumar

Anandan Pillai

Project Coordinator

Venitha Cutinho

Content Development Editor

Amey Varangaonkar

Copy Editors

Roshni Banerjee

Tanvi Bhatt

Karuna Narayanan

Cover Work

Simon Cardew

Proofreaders

Simran Bhogal

Maria Gould

Ameesha Green

Paul Hindle

Production Coordinator

Melwyn D'sa

Graphics

Abhinash Sahu

Acquisition Editor

Richard Gall

Foreword

I remember joining a company that was starting to use a tool that would forever change the way that sales was managed: a CRM that some of you might remember called Goldmine. The goal in using such a CRM was that the potential gold was in the data, and I, like countless salespeople before and after me, made sure that I made Goldmine part of my daily routine to both discover new opportunities as well as monitor the progress of my own pipeline. Back then, salespeople controlled the sales cycle and customers literally had to call or e-mail us to get access to critical business information they would need in order to decide whether or not they wanted to pursue a relationship with our company.

Fast forward to 2014, where one study suggests that 57% of the buying process is already completed by the time a potential customer contacts you. People are not only savvier at searching Google for information, but more and more professionals and decision makers are also spending more and more time in social media, digging around for information and asking questions from their network about who they should do business with. Engaging with and making business sense out of these social media profiles and conversations is becoming a challenging task for sales professionals.

This is the reality we see in 2014. However, some things have not changed. Just as this book is a no-fluff approach to what some perceive as a potentially abstract subject that could be a waste of time with no business ROI, I want to point out that social media replaces nothing yet complements everything. Business has always been—and will continue to be—about relationships. I like to say that social media and tools like Social CRM are an example of *New Tools, Old Rules*. Yet, with so many people spending so much time in social media, and becoming reliant on it for trustworthy information, social media becomes a place where we can both build and nourish a relationship while also uncovering business opportunities.

If you've never developed business in social media, ask your salespeople (or if you don't have any salespeople, ask sales professionals in your network) if LinkedIn (or any other social network) has contributed either directly or indirectly to business. You might be surprised by how many people will say there has been a contribution, and we already know that 78% of salespeople who use social media outsell those who don't.

I have personally developed business just by maintaining a regular presence on Twitter (inbound lead generation) as well as engaging in a timely and relevant manner on LinkedIn (outbound lead generation). We all know that conversations can lead to a very many different number of directions, but sometimes those seemingly random conversations and questions that we spot in social media can provide us with business opportunities.

On the other hand, there is no better way to keep in touch with clients and nourish customer relationships than with social media. Instead of relying on a monthly phone call or quarterly face-to-face meeting, we can literally be engaging with our client database on a daily basis wherever we might be in the world.

The challenge, though, is that time is a finite resource while Social Big Data (Big Data generated from social media) is seemingly infinite. When salespeople spot a conversation in social media, they need to quickly tie that conversation together to a user profile, gauge the relevance and context of the conversation, and quickly decide what their next step would be and execute. Traditional CRMs simply cannot, and were not designed to, monitor real-time conversations and engagement. On the other hand, it is simply inefficient to have your salespeople (or yourself) trying to piece data together among different tabs open in a browser and make business sense of what they are seeing.

Like Craig, I am also a Nimble user, and as a sample of what a Social CRM can deliver, you can quickly see not only the efficiency of having all of this information together in one dashboard, but also the tremendously relevant data about people that would simply be missed if you couldn't see all of the information in one place. I always say that navigating to a decision maker's LinkedIn profile is like virtually visiting their office in that it reveals a great deal about that person, the journey they have walked from a professional perspective, and common professional connections you might have with them. That information, however, is only one part of the picture: supplementing that data with input from other social networks such as Facebook and Twitter give us a more complete picture of that individual. Finally, mapping all of this information together with our own customer database gives you a sense of the power of utilizing a Social CRM as your primary business dashboard. I didn't even mention that a Social CRM will also allow you to engage with said individual on the right platform at the right time.

We already have data that indicates that 80% of salespeople who had access to LinkedIn profiles inside their Salesforce.com dashboard through the LinkedIn Sales Navigator product were able to find information that they would not have known otherwise. Apply this to also having access to other social networks in your dashboard and being able to engage with your clients or prospects wherever they are in social and you can feel the potential power that a Social CRM can have for your business.

Craig Jamieson, an expert for whom I have deep respect, will guide you through the process of choosing, implementing, and optimizing your Social CRM in a no-nonsense, ROI-driven manner. As you embark on utilizing a Social CRM, please don't forget how the concept *New Tools, Old Rules* will help you truly maximize your social presence and use a Social CRM for what it was intended: relationships. After all, social media was made for people, not businesses, right?

Neal Schaffer

Author of *Maximize Your Social, Wiley*
Founder of Maximize Social Business

About the Author

 **Craig M. Jamieson** is the managing member of Adaptive Business Services in Boise, Idaho, which also owns and operates NetWorks! Boise Valley B2B Networking Group.

Craig has been in B2B sales since 1977 and during that time, has served in a variety of positions including sales manager, division sales manager, national sales manager, district manager, and a business owner. He has also taught salesmanship at university level and has been self-employed since 2005 as a sales trainer and consultant.

Craig is a Nimble Social CRM and HootSuite Solution Partner, a TTI Performance Systems VAA, and he also provides training and consulting to businesses on how to leverage social sales tools, techniques, strategies, and Social CRM to increase their revenues. Craig currently writes a monthly column on social sales at http://maximizesocialbusiness.com/ and is presently a Midsize Insider who has been empowered to blog for IBM on the general topic of social business.

Craig first began using Contact Management software in the late 1980s. Today, Social CRM is the absolute hub of his sales and marketing efforts.

Please feel free to contact Craig via his website at www.adaptive-business.com. You can also find Craig on Twitter at @craigmjamieson and on LinkedIn at in/craigmjamieson.

Acknowledgments

I would very much like to thank and acknowledge the following people.

To God without whose intervention, I would likely be taking a dirt nap instead of writing this book.

To my wife, Denise, and my daughter, Alicia, who have put up with a lot over the years but have always shown me unconditional love and have remained supportive of my goals. I love you both very much!

To Neal Schaffer who has been a good friend and mentor and who also provided me with my first opportunity to write for a larger audience.

To Jennifer Harris who convinced me that I needed to start blogging and then kindly explained to me what a blog was.

To all of the members of NetWorks! Boise Valley who, whether they know it or not, have played a huge part in allowing me to grow professionally!

To all my clients and my friends… thank you for being there for me and allowing me to serve you!

About the Reviewers

Pramod Kumar has a decade plus of experience in managing sales, marketing, and customer service operations. He is an expert in business communications, operational management, sales and marketing, and building business strategies and road maps, Salesforce and marketing automation, and CRM implementation. He has worked with Fortune 500 companies managing customer service, sales, and marketing. He was VP sales for a major CRM manufacturer and has in-depth knowledge of developing and customizing CRM software as per business needs.

Pramod currently runs Inteleserv BPO Services (P) Ltd in Trivandrum, Kerala, India, which specializes in sales, marketing, CRM implementation, customer service, and outsourcing. He often visits college campuses to interact with students and budding entrepreneurs; he loves to talk about sales, marketing, and new age stakeholder relationship management. He loves technology and loves to live curious.

I would like to thank my wife, Jisha, who supported and encouraged me, especially during the review of this book. My sister, Nandini, had a special role to play in the review of this book. As a journalist and a writer, she was instrumental in checking whether the right message was being passed to readers.

Anandan Pillai works with HCL Technologies as a full-time digital consultant. Prior to this assignment, he used to lead social media duties at ZenithOptimedia (Publicis Groupe). He is a perfect blend of academician and practitioner. He is on the verge of completing a doctoral program and has published numerous research papers and management case studies at Harvard, Richard Ivey School, and so on to name a few. He published a book, *Social Media Simplified, Ocean Books*, which was one of the initial social media books in the Indian context and covered 30 social media case studies from various industries. He has a strong interest in digital marketing and has expertise in social media, content strategy, brand communities, and Social CRM. He loves conversing on Twitter (@anandan22) and is a regular blogger (www.anandanpillai.com).

Contents

Chapter 4: Define Your Social CRM Needs Prior to Any Investment 53

Chapter 9: Managing Your SCRM and Evaluating Your Investment 141

Appendix: Links 153

Preface

It was approximately 6 years ago that I was first introduced to the term and the concept of social media. At that time, the phrase itself made little sense, and I associated it with people on Twitter talking about what they had for breakfast or folks on Facebook sharing cute pictures of their children and pets. These uses struck me as a waste of my valuable time. Surely, there must be business-related applications for what appeared to be a promising new phenomenon. While large brands were quick to recognize the power and benefits of this medium, for the average company and small business in particular, acceptance of these ideas and practices took a little bit longer to formulate. Thankfully, this focus gradually began to take shape, and small businesses began to pay attention. As a business owner or manager, you are probably not interested in investing in something that, while novel, offers little more than that novelty. You are interested in results, nothing more and nothing less. Any investment that you make, and that is in terms of both time and money, needs to provide a return that is in excess of that investment, and this return is most easily measured by increased revenues.

Your business and customers have both evolved dramatically over the past several years. Much of this has to do with the explosion of the Internet and of social media specifically. Quite simply, buyer behaviors have changed, and smart businesses must learn to adapt to these changes. Certainly, there are challenges. More importantly, these shifts in your customers' behaviors represent opportunities for those companies who know how to find and then nurture them!

Whereas customers used to rely on your business and your sales and marketing staff to educate them on your product or service, many of these buyers are now doing this research on their own. They are going online, and even a simple Google search will provide them with much of the information that they seek. Moreover, they are asking and getting product recommendations from friends, family, and from people whom they know and trust, and they are using social networking as the preferred platform to secure these.

Prospective buyers are talking to each other, and they are talking about their needs and pain points. In some cases, they are even talking about you. What happens if you are not even there to listen and participate in these conversations? The answer is "nothing," and the result is the same. You will miss out on the opportunity to create a new customer or to further cement your relationship with an existing one.

About 4 years ago, I first recognized that there was an issue with traditional **CRM** (Customer Relationship Management). I was now talking to people on the social channels, but I had no way to track and monitor these conversations. So, I began to do the research for possible solutions and to write about my findings on this topic. While there were many *add-on* type products that would, for example, add a social layer to Outlook or Gmail, there were seemingly no CRMs that were designed to address this need. This has now changed!

Social CRM (SCRM), Social Customer Relationship Management, is the new breed of CRM which was itself preceded by what we called Contact Managers (CM) in the 1980s. Contact Managers focused on managing our customer and prospect data in the *3C* areas: contacts, calendars, and communications. While all of this data is very important, despite the name change to CRM, there remains absolutely no *relationship* element to be found in these legacy applications. The focus of traditional CRM has remained on data rather than on people. For many, it is little more than an electronic rolodex.SCRM, on the other hand, places relationships in the front and center in the company/buyer process. Think about this. Business has always been based on relationships. As consumers, we buy from those who we know, like, and trust. Relationships are developed by getting to know our customer and their needs. It comes from assisting them to get more from your product or service. It is secured by placing their needs above your own. We educate more than we sell. We make every effort to stay in touch consistently. Relationships in business are absolutely no different than those found in our personal lives. We show them the love, and the effective use of Social CRM will allow you to do just that!

This book has been written in an easy-to-read and step-by-step practical format. I have written this for small business, because I am a small business and I am a small business that uses Social CRM as the absolute hub of my sales and marketing efforts. As someone who has served in the roles of salesperson, sales manager, and owner, I understand the needs of each and the psychology of sales personnel in particular. Each chapter will include helpful tips and action items for you to take prior to moving to the next step in the process.

What this book covers

Chapter 1, Exploring the Key Benefits of Social CRM for Your Small Business: By the end of this chapter, you should haveu a solid understanding of Social CRM basics and how these might be deployed in your small business. This will be critical as in our next chapter; you will be laying the groundwork with your team to begin the discussion of Social CRM, which will then be followed by defining your needs and finally choosing and implementing your system.

Chapter 2, Social Business – the Foundation of Social CRM: Social Business is the business-related application of social media (LinkedIn, Facebook, Twitter, Google+, and so on), and this concept is the very foundation, the supporting structure that we find under Social CRM (SCRM). You have determined that SCRM may be right for you. We'll define *Social Business* and then discuss the four major social networks and how each can be applied to your small business.

Chapter 3, Laying the Groundwork for Social CRM: By this point, you should have a solid fundamental understanding of Social Business and how Social CRM (SCRM) will allow you to manage and leverage these fantastic new opportunities! This chapter will describe the first steps that you will you want to take to prior to choosing your product or even thinking about implementing it. In fact, these steps will help ensure the right choice of a Social CRM, it's successful implementation, and your business being able to realize the long-term benefits of this system

Chapter 4, Define Your Social CRM Needs Prior to Any Investment: Understanding your needs and goals today and anticipating your future needs will be critical elements in choosing which SCRM will ultimately be right for you. Without a clear vision of your needs, the features that you will require, and how you plan to use your SCRM, choosing your platform will be difficult at best. Your business is unique, and we will help you define what that means in terms of your ultimate SCRM selection.

Chapter 5, Choosing and Implementing Your New Social CRM: There are many choices out there, and you need to be able to filter through the mass of information in order to determine the right SCRM for you today as well as one that will be able to effectively scale for your anticipated growth and which will also be able to accommodate your additional application needs. This chapter includes helping you make your choice of vendor and support options. When it comes to actually implementing your system, will you do it yourself or will you want help? Regardless, there are a number of critical steps that you will want to take prior to your SCRM going live, including creating custom information fields, data cleansing and import, and user training.

Chapter 6, Training and SCRM Best Practices: In order to gain the most value from your new system, you must establish routines for its use. Through repetition, you establish a foundation for success, which we can then continue to build upon. Haphazard and unstructured usage will render your investment useless. This chapter will focus on the most common application of basic CRM features in your business, but it all starts and ends with great training!

Chapter 7, Exploring the Social Elements of SCRM: An SCRM is a CRM that adds a social layer, and SCRM is what adds the *relationship* into a CRM. The key to building relationships and uncovering opportunities will be your willingness to engage with others. This social element of SCRM will result in increased revenues.

Chapter 8, Enhancing Your Social CRM with Third-Party Applications and Integrations: Most SCRMs today are as much platforms as they are applications. This means that you can integrate them with many third-party applications in order to expand and enhance their capabilities. Some of these might include proposal preparation, advanced pipeline management, and marketing automation. We'll discuss these applications and many more.

Chapter 9, Managing Your SCRM and Evaluating Your Investment: We'll begin this chapter with a short recap of our previous discussions, and then we will move on to our suggestions to manage your system day to day as well as key things to consider as you evaluate your investment. Finally, we'll wrap it all up with a few closing thoughts and tips to ensure that your new Social CRM will deliver maximum results.

Appendix, Links: We will have discussed several applications during the course of this book, and the appendix will include links to all of them.

Who this book is for

If you are a small business owner, a sales manager, a salesperson, or even a solo entrepreneur who is looking for ways to significantly increase your revenues, this book is written specifically for you! As a small business, you likely wear many hats. While these varied responsibilities should be working together in concert, we often find ourselves fractured and disorganized. On top of that, we are busier than ever, and despite our best efforts, we have never managed to squeeze more than 24 hours out of a day. This guide will help you maximize your productive hours.

Ultimately, your single biggest challenge is generating new revenues from both your existing customers as well as your prospective ones and this book has been designed to show you how both can be accomplished with the deployment of SCRM. Wouldn't it be great to have one central location that will serve as the hub of your sales and marketing efforts? How wonderful would it be to discover and nurture new customers who do not even currently fall within your circles of influence? Wouldn't it be nice to have a stream of customers who are coming to you instead of you always having to prospect for them? Regarding your existing clients, will they buy more from you? Are they providing you with the quantity and quality of referrals that you would like to see? All of these are specific benefits that we will discuss within the pages of this book.

You might be thinking, *"What I do now seems to be working alright"*. That's wonderful because SCRM is designed to take what you do well now and make you even better at doing it! SCRM is not magic, but it will take your sales and marketing efforts to the next level. SCRM works because it makes sense, and we will do our best to remove any mystery that might be surrounding it! Let's get started!

Please note that we will be discussing many SCRM features but that not all of these features will be available in every vendor's SCRM. As I am a Nimble Social CRM Solution Partner, screenshots will be shown from this platform for example purposes, but this is not to say that Nimble is the only or even the best choice for your specific business and for your specific needs.

Conventions

In this book, you will find a number of styles of text that distinguish between different kinds of information. Here are some examples of these styles, and an explanation of their meaning.

New terms and **important words** are shown in bold.

Make a note

Warnings or important notes appear in a box like this.

Tip

Tips and tricks appear like this.

Reader feedback

Feedback from our readers is always welcome. Let us know what you think about this book—what you liked or may have disliked. Reader feedback is important for us to develop titles that you really get the most out of.

To send us general feedback, simply send an e-mail to feedback@impacktpub.com, and mention the book title via the subject of your message.

If there is a book that you need and would like to see us publish, please send us a note via the **Submit Idea** form on https://www.impacktpub.com/#!/bookidea.

Piracy

Piracy of copyright material on the Internet is an ongoing problem across all media. At Packt, we take the protection of our copyright and licenses very seriously. If you come across any illegal copies of our works, in any form, on the Internet, please provide us with the location address or website name immediately so that we can pursue a remedy.

Please contact us at copyright@impacktpub.com with a link to the suspected pirated material.

We appreciate your help in protecting our authors, and our ability to bring you valuable content.

1

Exploring the Key Benefits of Social CRM for Your Small Business

Your decision to add Social CRM to your business has the potential to pay you, your people, your customers, and your company enormous dividends! We want to help ensure your success, and investing in this book is a great way to start. In the enclosed chapters, we are going to walk you step by step through the entire business process of choosing and implementing your new Social CRM. Let's get started!

By the end of this chapter, you should have a solid understanding of the basics of Social CRM and how it might be deployed in your small business. This will be critical, as in the subsequent chapters, you will be laying the groundwork with your team to begin the discussion of Social CRM. This will then be followed by defining your needs and finally choosing and implementing your system.

In this chapter, we will explore the following topics:

> ➤ The Social Media Ecosystem
> ➤ Social building blocks
> ➤ Why a Social CRM?
> ➤ Social sales
> ➤ Social marketing
> ➤ Social customer service
> ➤ Managing your business with Social CRM

Your success with Social CRM can be quantified in a number of ways, including new revenues, increased lead generation, as well as by customer service and retention. While many of your company departments will utilize Social CRM as a tool to meet their individual goals, all departments working together will ensure that your overall targets of increasing revenues and exceeding customer expectations are realized.

The social media ecosystem

The *Social Media Ecosystem* is one of the ways in which we can envision how the seemingly disparate parts of the social channels and your small business can and will work together. By some definitions, it might be considered to be a living and breathing organism with each part feeding the other and vice versa. As a result of this, your small business brand messaging has the ability to be widely distributed throughout the ecosystem (social networks).

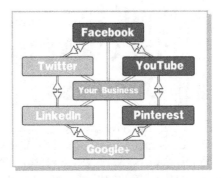

In the preceding figure, the satellites that surround your business are shown. They represent the various social networks, and as you can see, each of the social networks is pointing toward your business. Traffic generated from each network can be directed to your landing pages, blog articles, and literally any place that you would like your customers and prospective customers to visit. It gets even better!

Your business marketing assets (articles, white papers, and so on) can also be leveraged as the source of this shared information, which gives you the ability to distribute important messages out to each of the social channels; this will then, in turn, direct traffic back to your business. Each of these channels can also be used to share information with another network and then to either point back to the originating network or directly to your business.

For example, you could share your LinkedIn profile on Twitter and then have readers click the link to follow back to your LinkedIn profile, which will, in turn, link to your company page on LinkedIn. You might, for example, share a link that offers a free e-book and have that link direct to a landing page on your website, where contact information is captured and a record is automatically created in your SCRM for follow-up by sales or customer service. Linking is the key element that is used to direct people to the information that we wish them to be exposed to.

Social building blocks

We call your marketing assets *social building blocks*. While Social CRM is the tool that we will use to aggregate and manage our customer-focused activities, it is the *social building blocks* that will enable the activities themselves. These activities will also go a very long way toward establishing your expertise and making that visible to others. By providing a perceived value to your networks, you attract others to you and your company.

A good example of this would be posts (blog articles) and pages on your website. Assuming that your company has stories to share with your customers and prospective customers, you should and you will also want to put these in writing by way of a blog. In this way, this information is available at all times. Blog articles work for you continuously and unattended. Other articles, even those not written by you, that pertain to your business or to the products and services that you offer will also go a very long way in establishing your company's expertise.

Other examples of social building blocks would include the following:

➤ Newsletters and other campaigns

➤ Images including slideshows and photos

➤ Mentions of your business or of its personnel that are found on other sites

➤ LinkedIn, Facebook, and Google+ company pages

➤ LinkedIn, Facebook, and Google+ groups that you manage or frequent

➤ Your LinkedIn, Twitter, Facebook, and Google+ profiles and those of your company personnel

➤ Your company's video channel on YouTube

The social networks themselves represent both the power and challenge that is associated with social business. Each is actually a separate communication channel much like the phone or e-mail. People are talking to each other on these networks, and they also want to talk with you and your company. What happens if you are not there? Nothing.

Why a Social CRM?

While a traditional CRM is the best way to organize your contact information (companies and people) in a central location, SCRM will provide you with an additional organizational layer that addresses the social media activities within your small business. As a social business, you will be conversing with your customers and prospective customers on various social channels, and there are four main ways to do this. They are as follows:

1. Visit each network regularly. Go to the home page of each social network on a regular basis and look for messages and opportunities to engage.

2. Use a good *social dashboard* such as Hootsuite to monitor these networks from a single location.

3. Make use of analytical tools such as Google Analytics in order to monitor and track visitor activities (and social sources) on your website(s).

4. Deploy SCRM in your small business that may have the conversational capabilities of a social dashboard combined with the contact record-keeping abilities that are found in a CRM.

Why would you want to have the ability to track and monitor conversations? The simple answer would be for the same reasons that you maintain file folders for your accounts and you are loath to deleting messages from your e-mail inbox. Efficient and effective small businesses need to have some sort of a paper trail, a record of their activities, to refer back to.

As a long-time CRM user, I love that my e-mail conversations and my notes are a part of an electronic contact record. My memory just isn't that good. As somebody who is active on social media, it would be almost impossible to keep my conversations and communications, not to mention my engagement opportunities, separated and organized without an SCRM.

Regardless of where your social activities take place (smartphone, laptop, tablet, desktop), those relevant activities should be captured by your SCRM. This also holds true regardless of which platforms (the social networks or third-party applications) are being used. If it is social, it all ties back to the networks themselves which, in turn, feed these conversations to your SCRM and other third-party applications.

From the standpoint of effective use of your time and the ability to keep **ALL** of this information in one location, SCRM is the obvious choice. More so, *engagements lead to relationships and relationships result in revenues*. This is the long-standing formula that is found in real life, and the same equation is applied to social business.

SCRM is also largely about *discovery*. Every day, people are talking on the social networks about their needs and their pain points. While you may not be able to listen in to a conversation about your company that is being conducted face-to-face by your next-door neighbors, social monitoring will allow you to discover these conversations regardless of where they are taking place. You will then be able to create and assign tasks to follow up on these and then begin to build a relationship with that person which may result in a sale.

As social media itself is based on the *law of attraction* rather than *interruption*, you will also have the ability to draw others to you as opposed to you going out and finding them or having to walk into their places of business or personal lives, unannounced and unexpected.

In the article, "IBM Reveals Their Predictions About The Future Of Social Customer Relationship Management (CRM)," the author interviews Sandesh Bhat who is the VP of Web and Unified Collaboration Software for IBM Collaboration Solutions:

> *"We believe Social CRM – the integration of social media and analytics with customer relationship management strategies – is the next frontier for organizations that want to exploit the power of social media to get closer to customers, old and new. Social networking sites (e.g. Facebook, LinkedIn), micro blogging capabilities (Twitter, Jaiku), media sharing capabilities (YouTube, SlideShare), social bookmarking sites (Digg, Delicious), and review sites (Yelp, Trip Advisor) will play a crucial and important role in successfully transforming sales."*

Now is a good time to begin thinking about what your goals for SCRM might be. While we will define these in more detail in our upcoming chapters, having a good understanding of your overall goals and the benefits that you would hope to achieve by reaching these will be critical elements in your discussions with your other team members.

Key benefits of Social CRM

As we explore some of the key benefits of Social CRM, we must stress that SCRM is a complex, relatively new, and rapidly evolving market. This does not mean that it should be difficult to use or to deploy. *What it does mean is that not all features will be offered by all vendors*, and even then, the overall functionality of a particular feature that is offered might also differ largely by vendor. As such, it is very difficult to provide specific examples.

This section is designed to provide you with a good overall view of what SCRM might do for you; it will help ensure that when you finally make your choice of a vendor, you don't discover after the fact that "Oh, I thought that I was getting ... this?"

These are general benefits. It is not the goal or the purpose of this book to tell you how to conduct a social marketing campaign or any other activity but rather to let you know that SCRM might very well be able to assist you in these efforts. We will look at these in more detail in one of the upcoming chapters when we discuss the best practices for day-to-day usage of SCRM.

Global benefits

Global benefits can be realized and leveraged by any team member regardless of function or department. If you feel that any item that appears in a single area would also apply to other departments of your small business (and you likely will), feel free to incorporate that!

Customer retention

We will always place customer retention at the top of any list. The axiom that it is 10 times more expensive to find a new customer than it is to keep an existing one is not a myth. Your existing customers are the lifeblood of your business. They pay the bills, refer you to others, and become brand advocates and ambassadors. They also likely have the ability and the willingness to spend more money with your company. Why do customers leave? Here are some recent statistics:

1. They die (1%)
2. They move (3%)
3. They are taken by one of your competitors (13%)
4. They are unhappy with the your product, service, or price (14%)
5. They felt ignored, mistreated, or unappreciated (69%)

We can't help you with death or relocation, but when SCRM is used properly, it will greatly assist you with minimizing points 3, 4, and 5, which comprise 96 percent of all lost customers!

Create new revenues

Our view is that everybody in a company sells. Marketing creates brand awareness and generates leads. Customer service takes an unhappy customer and converts them into a happy customer who buys more. The person who answers the phone sets the tone with that customer and they sell. Salespeople sell. These rules are applicable in a traditional environment and are no different in one that is social. However, a social environment will accelerate these efforts.

We create new revenues from both new and existing customers. We do so by targeting our connections to find the right people, using search to discover new opportunities, by tracking triggers that indicate potential opportunities, attracting new opportunities and connections to us, and by nurturing all of these into relationships that pay consistent and repeating dividends.

Contact records

Everything starts and ends with a contact (person or account) record. Contact records are the absolute nucleus of any good CRM or SCRM, and we would argue strongly against any application that claims to be either that does not have individual contact records. Mind you, many of these applications may be great at what they are designed to do (marketing automation, social dashboard, customer service, and so on). You may choose to use these in addition to your SCRM, or they may integrate directly with it, thereby providing you with a more complete solution if required.

What contact records allow you to do is to focus on that specific contact, your history with them, deals that you have in progress, tasks that need to be completed, and what they are discussing on their social networks. This capability alone will result in increased revenues!

Does this mean that you will create a contact record for every engagement that you will encounter on the social channels? No, you will create contact records for those accounts that have the potential of either doing business with you, referring you to a new business, or those that would provide another benefit that makes it worth keeping in touch with them.

Tip

Please note that screenshot images shown is this book are for reference purposes only.

Stay organized

Not everybody, including me, is a great file organizer. I could always manage to get the right pieces and scraps of paper into the correct folder(s). but that was about the extent of it. SCRM allows you to easily and electronically store and organize all of your notes, a record of your activities, exchanged communications, just about anything into an individual contact record. Furthermore, much (if not all of this) should be available to you virtually anywhere via a mobile app (if available) or your browser (if your SCRM is cloud-based).

With organization comes productivity and, more importantly, productivity that leads directly to revenue. Review your history of communications with that client before your next call instead of fumbling around trying to remember what and when you talked about last. Listen to what your customer is talking about now on the social networks and then incorporate those topics into your conversation.

Unified communications

Each contact record is a unified communications inbox or history. This means that right from within a contact record, I can see what, when, and **where** we have spoken in the past and quickly reply to communications as they arrive and are brought to my attention. **Where** is the key. Was it by e-mail, by phone, or by one or more of the social channels? Regardless, this information will be at your fingertips.

Calendar and task management

Schedule calendar events (one-time or recurring) and, if appropriate, invite other team members to attend. You will be also be able to create and assign tasks to other team members. This may include the ability to generate tasks directly from incoming e-mails and opportunities or customer needs that are gleaned from the social networks. Then, organize these tasks by type (meeting, phone call, send e-mails) to ensure the best use of your available time. Finally, create a system that will ensure that these tasks are completed correctly and in a timely manner.

Collaboration

Your new SCRM will likely allow you to set permission levels (who can do what within the system), but we would strongly encourage you to have things such as contacts, calendar, and tasks accessible to most, if not all team members. In this way, any team member should be able to update records with the most recent pertinent information. This might include the status of a task or project; questions for the team leader about a specific task or project; or even things such as useful pieces of information.

For example, seeing that the account manager has a lunch meeting with an important client, customer service might leave a note letting him know that the customer had a recent issue that is still being resolved and/or your assistant might note that says, "Enjoy lunch with Bob, and remember that he is a vegetarian!" You are a team. Leverage that!

Document storage and management

Documents might include copies of letters, estimates, and quotes. This may also include things such as marketing pieces and collateral. These items may be stored in a central depository for access by all or, in the case of estimates and quotes, attached to the contact record itself. Your SCRM may also have the ability to generate quotes and proposals from directly within the application itself, or there are a number of third-party applications that may facilitate this.

Leverages social sales

Social Sales builds upon what we would call the *relationship-selling* model. With social sales, we will incorporate the benefits of social networking into the selling process. It is important to note that social sales is meant to augment, not replace the more traditional selling model(s). That being said, social sales and Social CRM will allow us to effectively leverage the best of both!

Build relationships

Social relationships are formed in the exact manner in which they are nurtured in real life. Often, the basis to initiate a relationship is founded on the establishment of common interests. At the very least, knowing the interests of our customers and prospective customers, and sharing ours with them is one heck of a good start!

When I first started in B2B sales, I was expected to make 30 cold calls daily. Every time I called on a prospective customer, my eyes were darting and my ears were wide open. I was looking for those things that would provide me with clues to that buyer's interests and purchasing patterns. Today, we can do this, and more, from the comfort of our desks just by visiting LinkedIn and Facebook or by conducting a Google search.

Social CRM allows us to go even a few steps further. Many SCRMs will include a contact's *social streams* (what they are talking about on the social channels right now, and who they are talking to) directly within the contact records themselves. You can monitor these conversations, choose to engage if appropriate, and maybe uncover a new opportunity or connection in the process. Knowledge is power.

Make the touches

If you want to build, let alone even create, relationships, you have to make the touches. Everybody knows that, but how often do they get lost in the shuffle of daily activities? A lot. Touches can be made in person, by phone, by e-mail, and by regular mail. With social networking, we add to our list of options. We can now like, comment, engage, endorse, and connect these people to others thereby expanding their connections and potential opportunities.

SCRM will make it extremely easy to make sure that you do not miss these opportunities. You should be able to schedule specific call-back reminders along with what you are calling back about. You may also have the ability to schedule recurring reminders to stay in touch. One popular way to do this is by classifying your accounts as being either "A" (touch weekly), "B" (touch monthly), "C" (touch quarterly), and "D" (delete). You can determine your own schedules, but SCRM will remind you to make your touches on this schedule. Your SCRM may even remind you of the last time you contacted an account.

Combining scheduled touches with random touch opportunities (based on monitoring and engaging on social channels) is a winning combination that will produce increased revenues and customers who know that you appreciate them!

Generate referrals

Who wants referrals? You do. Referrals are *sales gold*. When you exceed customer expectations, and this is based on a number of levels and factors, you will earn referrals from these customers. You will have also *earned the right* to ask them for referrals.

Tip

Make the touches and make them count! Your best referrers, even if they themselves don't spend the most money with you, should be included in your "A" list.

Find new connections

The crux of social networking is that we want to connect with the people who are connected to the people that we are connected to. Call this the *relationship map*. If you go to someone's LinkedIn profile, you will see a map on the right sidebar that shows you how you are related to that person. You are not connected to them, but your friend Nancy is. Perhaps Nancy might introduce you. Facebook has a similar function as does Google+ and Twitter.

Some SCRMs are beginning to map these relationships for you. They are also making it very easy to send connection requests from within a contact record itself. For example, you are in Nancy's contact record, and you see that she is talking on Twitter to *@bigspender*. Hover your mouse over that person's handle to see their Twitter profile. If they look like the kind of person that you would like to follow, do so right there and then without leaving your SCRM.

As this is a person that you would like to follow up with later, you can click the button to add them as a contact and then schedule a touch reminder. You might even create a task for your assistant and ask them to research this person for you and then to attach their findings to the contact record.

Discover new opportunities

Both connections and identified needs/pain points represent opportunities; therefore, when we discover on the social channels that somebody we are connected to is speaking with somebody that we are not connected to, this potential new connection might become an opportunity. What about when they are discussing a potential need for our product or service? Now, we have a golden opportunity, and you can begin the engagement process and then follow that up with a connection request, a new contact record, and maybe even a lead and/or opportunity record within your SCRM. You are on your way!

Your SCRM may also allow you to search many social channel updates by keywords (words used to identify your brand, a competitor, a need, maybe even a sentiment). Searches can often be saved for reuse later on. Once a potential opportunity has been uncovered, the same rule to discover new connections applies.

Tip

Keep in mind that by providing value and demonstrating your expertise on the social channels, opportunities will also come to you. This is known as the "Law of Attraction".

Manage leads

Many SCRMs will have records for both leads and opportunities (deals). Leads are generally considered to be unqualified and would be assigned to a salesperson to determine whether or not there is a valid opportunity to be had. A qualified lead is then *converted* to an opportunity. Leads are often generated by marketing, and you, as a manager or owner, will want to have the ability to assign these leads and, more importantly, be assured that they are being followed up and followed through on.

Pipeline management

Your pipeline (forecast, funnel) should give you an accurate portrayal of deals (opportunities) in progress, a predicted dollar value, what stage they are in in the sales process, a weighted deal value that is determined by the percentage chance of closing (based on the sales stage) being applied against the dollar value, and a projected close date. Ultimately, deals are either won, lost, or deleted. SCRM is very effective at managing your pipeline and will keep these deals front and center to ensure that they do not fall through the cracks.

Regardless of whether it is a win or a loss, we also want to know *why*. If we can identify patterns for success, we want to duplicate those. If we have patterns to our losses, we need to rectify those. If we consistently win deals on the basis of being low bid, we may be leaving cash on the table or, conversely, are our prices too high for the market or compared to our competition?

Tip

In order to have effective pipeline management program, you must keep each deal updated with its most current status, including dollar value, percentage chance of closing, and sales stage.

Social marketing

An interesting discussion, and particularly as it relates to small business, is that the lines between sales and marketing are blurring. Part of this is due to the fact that as a small business, your sales and marketing staff may be joined together. The social channels have also had a dramatic effect on marketing. All personnel are, to some extent at least, involved in actively creating brand awareness and often via their own personal networks. Everybody markets, and this is good for your business!

Create brand awareness and brand monitoring

One of the primary responsibilities of marketing is to create brand awareness, that is, how customers perceive our company's name and what things they associate with that. Is it quality? Fun? Another part of this is brand monitoring, that is, what people are saying about us on the Internet.

If the comments are positive, marketing might reward that individual and thank them for being a brand advocate. This might also be a lead for sales to follow up on. If the sentiment is negative, this conversation might be forwarded to customer service for their review and resolution.

Your Social CRM might enable you to perform many of these functions from within the SCRM itself. It can be used to create the updates that promote the brand (remember social building blocks) and also monitor your brand via network keyword search operatives.

Manage campaigns

While there are Social CRMs available that will allow you to create and manage marketing campaigns, these are generally limited to things such as e-mail blasts, unless the SCRM is very robust and more designed for an enterprise-level company compared to a small business. E-mail campaigns should naturally attach themselves to contact records in your SCRM. SCRM can certainly help you track your ROI ((Return on Investment) on specific campaigns.

This being said, this function is also a very popular one for SCRM third-party integrations with marketing automation companies such as HubSpot and Marketo. Generally, this does include some level of syncing between the two applications. For example, a HubSpot integration with an SCRM might create a tab and customized fields within an SCRM contact record, and this section will display the data associated with that application, such as lead scoring, the number of times this person has visited our website and where they went, and the marketing collateral offers that they have responded to and downloaded.

Generate leads

Another primary function of marketing is to generate leads that can be distributed to the appropriate team for follow-up. This will often include the development of effective *landing pages* on your website along with some sort of *call-to-action* (CTA), which invites visitors to provide their e-mail address and other contact information in return for generally receiving some sort of free offer. Such offers might include an e-book, white papers, or entry into a drawing contest. It is generally quite easy to create an integration between that contact form and your SCRM. This is commonly known as *web-to-lead*.

Contact forms on my website will accept your information, send me an e-mail notification of your visit and/or request, allow you to download an offer if there is one, create a record for you in my SCRM, tag (group) you as a website lead, and will finally add you to my mailing list with a double opt-in verification. This is all completed automatically.

However, there are other important aspects to generating leads. Marketing will want to know if leads are, in fact, being followed up on and will also want feedback from sales regarding the quality of the leads that are being distributed; SCRM can help with both.

Create and manage groups, communities, and pages

Pages and groups that are found on LinkedIn, Facebook, and Google+ are typically considered to be the domain of marketing, so creating and managing these presences is the natural fit. These areas also have the advantage of being frequented by people who have already opted into your company message.

In this case, the function of marketing is to create an engaging environment that will lead to direct connections on that platform, which will have the potential to convert to paying customers if they are not already. At this point, contact records will be created in your SCRM for a more individually focused marketing/sales approach.

Social customer service

Customer service technology combined with your customer's expectations of how, when, and where to receive support, have both changed dramatically! Customers are asking for and are expecting immediate responses to service requests that have been initiated on social networks.

Online reputation management

The preceding example of my experience of receiving customer support via Twitter highlights another very critical element that has been brought forth via social media and the Internet. Prior to this, the only people who were aware of an unhappy customer experience were limited to the customer, the company if they even brought this to their attention, and to friends who they shared this poor experience with.

If good news has always traveled fast and bad news even quicker, now both are moving at light speed through the social networks, because any comment that any customer can make (good or bad) has the potential to be amplified by others who see it and will happily forward that message to their networks.

You simply must be prepared to monitor and respond appropriately to all of your business brand mentions that will be discovered on the social networks, and Social CRM will greatly assist you with this task. Not doing so or doing so poorly could very well prove to be disastrous for you and your small business.

Customer support

As discussed earlier, smart companies monitor the social channels for brand mentions. Twitter has the ability to include some sentiment (happy, sad, mad) filtering, and there are many third-party apps that will utilize much more sophisticated algorithms, which we will look at more closely later. Dedicated customer support applications that will integrate with many SCRMs are numerous!

Some companies have gone as far as setting up specific Twitter accounts for customer support, and they have also set up areas on their company pages (Facebook, LinkedIn, Google+) specifically for the purpose of support. Even if you do not have a dedicated space on your pages, you will still wish to closely monitor these areas. As such, pages and groups may be managed by both marketing and support

The suggested steps to providing effective support in combination with your SCRM are as follows:

1. Monitor your social channels via keyword searches for brand mentions, and when relevant mentions are discovered, engage and offer your assistance or thank them for their support.

2. Decide what type of support is required. Is this a question or an issue for support or is it a question better suited for sales or marketing?

3. If for support, create a case record on your SCRM. If your SCRM does not offer cases, create a contact record, tag it for support, and assign it to a specialist.

4. If for sales or marketing, forward the conversation via e-mail to the appropriate party and/or create a task for follow-up.

Solidify relationships

Ultimately, the goal of any support department is to retain customers and to solidify relationships. *Customer service issues are quite often opportunities in disguise.* Studies have consistently demonstrated that when a customer has an issue and that issue is resolved in a timely and correct fashion, you will have a much stronger customer relationship than you would have had if that issue had never even occurred in the first place.

Manage your business

While the bottom line is the ultimate indicator of success or failure, by keeping your fingers on the pulse of your business, you will be able to track progress and head off challenges before they become overwhelming and damaging. More importantly, you will have a firm understanding of what it is that makes you successful so that you can duplicate it!

As a small business owner or manager, you likely have a number of concerns. You want to have the ability to identify your top performers as well as why and where others may be struggling. If you have multiple profit centers, you will want to see the forecasted and actual numbers from each. Are your customers being serviced properly, what issues are being raised, and are there patterns to these issues that need to be addressed?

Perhaps, most importantly, your ability as a small business to be able to quickly evaluate these areas, pinpoint trouble spots, and then to make any needed adjustments might be the difference between ultimately being profitable or having to report a loss. While larger businesses may be able to weather such storms, smaller businesses do not generally have this luxury!

Your SCRM should provide you with the ability to look at individual contact records, activities, funnels, or just about any other metric by teams and by individual team members. However, let's begin by stating the obvious. When it comes to data, if garbage goes in, garbage comes out. If nothing goes in, nothing comes out. Therefore, for reports (or for **anything** related to SCRM) to have any value at all, it is paramount that data be entered accurately and consistently!

Most SCRMs will come with an assortment of preconfigured reports. Common report variations would include the following:

- *Sales* (by company, team, and by individual)
  - Won/loss reports
  - Sales activity reports
  - Sales forecast/pipeline/funnel opportunities by stage or by type
  - Opportunities by lead source and leads by lead source
- *Marketing* (by campaign and overall)
  - Campaign results
  - Conversion rates, opening rates, and click rates
- *Customer Service* (by company, team, and individual)
  - Open cases
  - Resolved cases
  - Cases by type
  - Time to resolve cases

You will quite likely want to see specific information, formatted in a certain manner, which is unique to your business model. Many SCRMs will allow you to create custom fields that can be used to store this data and then to create custom reports that will allow you to aggregate it.

Summary

In this chapter, we discussed some of the key benefits of Social CRM. SCRM has both global applications (utilized by all departments) as well as department-specific applications. When used consistently and properly, SCRM will help you exceed customer expectations and increase your revenues. Here are the key points to take away from this chapter:

> ➤ By effectively deploying your social building blocks, you will begin to leverage the Social Media Ecosystem, and you will establish your company and your people as leaders in your industry. As people still do buy from people, and this will place you in a unique position to capitalize on these opportunities, and SCRM will allow you to manage these toward their greatest chances for success.

> ➤ Furthermore, social networking is as much about *being found* as it is about *finding*. You will attract others to your business, and the people who you will attract will very likely have already qualified you as someone who they would like to do business with! While social networking and SCRM will augment, not replace, your traditional sales, marketing, and customer service efforts, it will make you better at what you already do!

> ➤ All of these activities will lead to collaboration and that is both internal (within your company) and external (with your customers and prospective customers). With collaboration comes alignment, and when this occurs, your messaging will be consistent across all channels and by all parties!

In our next chapter, we will begin the process of selecting your new SCRM, and this starts with laying the groundwork with your teams before making the move to Social CRM. This chapter should provide you with a good foundation for your discussions. In fact, you might have other key people read the same chapter so that they too will have a good fundamental understanding of what it is that you hope to achieve!

>2
Social Business – the Foundation of Social CRM

Social Business is the business-related application of social media (LinkedIn, Facebook, Twitter, Google+, and so on), and this concept is the very foundation, the supporting structure that we find under **Social CRM** (**SCRM**). My definition, which is a compilation of commonly found definitions for *Social Business*, would be as follows:

> *"A social business integrates social media tools and strategies, internally and externally, with the goal of enhancing the customer experience and exceeding customer expectations in a seamless fashion regardless of communication channels. It leverages these technologies to become more effective in those key areas that it already focuses on in real life."*

In this chapter, we will do the following:

- ➤ Define *Social Business*
- ➤ Provide overviews of the four main social networks

Let's begin by analyzing each segment of our *Social Business* definition:

- ➤ **A social business integrates social media tools and strategies, internally and externally**: Social media tools and strategies are critical concepts. Social CRM is a tool. Your social networks are also tools. What you wish to do with them (your goals and objectives), how you will take the steps needed to accomplish your tasks (deploy your tools), and how you will track and monitor your results are all key elements of social strategy.

- ➤ **Integration correctly implies that social business must become a part of the fabric that makes up your company**: Social business is a part of your company culture that will be found in each and every department. Not only does social business apply externally (customer facing), it also applies internally (company facing).

➤ **The goal of enhancing the customer experience and exceeding customer expectations**: The customer experience is what your clients envision when they think about doing business with your company. Is it pleasant? Is it fun? Is it painful? The customer experience is one of the key areas where you can truly separate yourself from your competitors. Most often, the customer experience will be largely dictated by whether or not you have managed to exceed your customer's expectations. Make no mistake about this. There are only three possible results of a customer interaction with you and with your company, and they are *did not meet, met*, or *exceeded* customer expectations. *Did not meet* is self-explanatory. *Met* is, at best, a neutral experience. There was nothing, either good or bad, that was worth remembering. *Exceeding* customer expectations should be the **only** acceptable outcome.

➤ **In a seamless fashion regardless of communication channels**: *Seamless* refers to that which appears to be natural and consistent, and *communication channels* refer to where this activity is taking place, that is, in person, by phone, via e-mail, or on social networks.

➤ **It leverages these technologies to become more effective in those key areas that it already focuses on in real life**: One core concept of being a social business is that it does not make you different or something that you are currently not. What it does do is magnify that which you already are. Therefore, if you are a business that is already known for providing a quality product and service, social business will **amplify** this reputation. Amplification is realized by leveraging the *reach* of social media, which is achieved by one person passing on information to potentially millions of others via social networks (Twitter, Facebook, LinkedIn, Google+, and others).

As a social business, your SCRM will allow you to leverage a six-step engagement process with your customers:

1. Monitor social networks for conversations regarding you and/or your product and also for discussions related to the solutions that you provide
2. Listen to and evaluate the conversation to determine if entering this discussion would be appropriate and pertinent
3. Enter the conversation (engage) if that is considered to be appropriate
4. Follow through based on determined needs and begin to develop a relationship
5. Continue to nurture this relationship and this opportunity
6. Constantly and consistently work together as a team to exceed customer expectations

Who do people buy from? They generally buy from those that they like, trust, know, and respect. Social networking provides a unique opportunity to demonstrate and solidify your standing in all of these key areas!

A social business moves away from *the pitch* and solidly toward conversation. We are not there to sell to our customers in the traditional sense. We gain and secure customers through education, getting to know them better, and making them a part of our team rather than a folder in our file cabinet. Social networking does not replace our traditional activities; it augments them and makes them better!

Understanding Social CRM

The major difference between traditional CRM and Social CRM is that SCRM integrates our social networking activities within the CRM itself. Therefore, as a social business, you have to be active, or be willing to become active, on social networking platforms in order for this to have any real value.

This being said, make no mistake in understanding that there is a huge difference between having a presence on these networks, being active on them, and being productive on each. As our goal is to increase our revenues, we need to be able to do the following:

> ➤ Target the right connections
> ➤ Discover new revenue opportunities
> ➤ Initiate and then build relationships
> ➤ Convert these relationships into revenues

These networks (also called channels) are the social core of any SCRM. Activities that occur on these networks are mined and captured from the networks themselves, and this information is then brought into and organized within your SCRM. In other words, let's say that you engage directly with somebody on Twitter. Your SCRM will recognize this conversation, identify who you are conversing with, find that person's record within the SCRM (or allow you to create one), and then will add this conversation to that person's record. See the following example of a unified message box on a contact record. You will see one e-mail, two LinkedIn private messages, and a LinkedIn profile update.

The really great thing about social networking is that it allows us to not only find new customers (outbound prospecting), it also allows us to attract new customers (inbound discovery). *We attract others by being real, interesting, and providing a perceived value such as knowledge and tips about our products and services.*

While SCRM will help us manage our social activities, there will be times when you will need to be on the social networks themselves. Therefore, it is critical that we have a solid understanding of each and how best to leverage them for our purposes. While this is not a book on social media, we do want to give you a very brief overview of each of the four major social networks. You will also find a link at the back of this book that will allow you to download the *2014 CMO's Guideline to the Social Media Landscape*, which will provide you with great tips about the effectiveness of the six most popular networks.

Network overviews

It is important that we point out that it is not necessary for your company and its people to be active on every social network. The most important thing is that you be active on those channels where your contacts (customers and prospects) are active. For example, while many might consider LinkedIn to be the preferred network for B2B (business-to-business) companies, others may feel that Facebook may be the same for those companies that are B2C (business to consumer). These are not hard and fast rules, and we will discuss this in more depth in *Chapter 3, Laying the Groundwork for Social CRM*.

LinkedIn

LinkedIn is widely considered to be **the** social business network. One important thing to keep in mind with every network is that we will want to ensure that all of our activities will be appropriate for that specific network. In the case of LinkedIn, the social relationship object is business, which means that you might want to share your messages that are in a business context.

LinkedIn is fairly straightforward, but there are certain areas that you will want to pay close attention to in order to maximize your effectiveness with this platform. Much of what we discuss on LinkedIn will also be applicable to our other networks, and as LinkedIn is the business network, we will spend most of this chapter's discussion here. You will also notice that many of the networks will offer very similar features that have, in fact, been *borrowed* (copied) from another channel.

Tip

Please note that, as of this writing, LinkedIn has recently made the decision to remove access to its platform from all CRM/SCRM systems with the exception of Salesforce and Microsoft. This decision is also affecting some other sales-related applications that would not be classified as being either a CRM or a Social CRM. Therefore, whatever integration that you will find with LinkedIn may be extremely limited. This decision, of course, may be reversed at some point.

Twitter

If the social context of LinkedIn is business, the social context of Twitter is just about anything. Whereas LinkedIn is the company boardroom, Twitter is likened to a cocktail party. Twitter is fast and furious, and it is very easy to maintain and be active on. Much of this is based on its 140-character update limit. It is very strong when it comes to reach (having your messages viewed by a high number of people) and information exchange. Twitter is a great way to meet new interesting people (potential customers), engage with them, and then (if appropriate) move your relationship to the next level. For example, begin your engagement on Twitter and then follow-up with a request to connect on LinkedIn.

Facebook

Facebook may be best described as the *neighborhood BBQ*. It is where friends and family gather and share largely personal stories. This is not to say that marketers do not make effective use of Facebook. On the contrary, some marketers use Facebook as their primary source for revenue-generating activities. The secret is that they use Facebook's natural affinity for conversation and images to make their brand messages both fun and personal. Friends buy from friends, and friends do not deliver hard sales pitches to other friends.

As Facebook is where you show your *human side*, it is best to follow the 80/20 rule, with 80 percent being keeping your topics light and no more than 20 percent of your activity being devoted to business. This can present a quandary to some people who wish to market on Facebook. How do you mix business and pleasure? Do I want my business customers to see the same updates that I share with my nieces and nephews? That's a fair question. Fortunately, we will discuss a solution for this later on in this chapter.

Google+

When Google+ was first introduced, the buzz was that it was designed to be "the Facebook killer". This was similar to what had been said about its predecessor, Google Buzz, and the product called Wave that followed it. Neither was as successful as many predicted them to be, and both were shelved prior to even complete introductions. Given this track record, why should we pay attention to Google+?

Google+ is a beautifully designed product, and you can't ignore the fact that it is from Google that also controls a very healthy share of search, e-mail, video, images, shopping, online storage, and the list goes on and on. Will it be the *Facebook killer*? Perhaps, but not likely in my opinion. Mind you, I like Google+! The challenge is that people who are entrenched on Facebook will stay there until they are given compelling reasons to move to another platform, and those reasons for most are just not there, at least not yet.

Your personal profiles and company pages

Profiles and company pages tell people who you are, what you do, and what you specialize in. As in real life, there are no second chances to make a good first impression!

LinkedIn

LinkedIn members actually have two profiles:

> ➤ Your full profile is viewable by first-degree connections only

> ➤ Your public profile (you can control what is shown) is viewable by everyone who is not a first-degree connection

Your profile on LinkedIn is both your online resume and your inbound marketing tool, and first impressions do count! When your prospective customers are looking on LinkedIn for people who have the potential to fulfil their needs, will they find you? And then, if they do, what will they find? The reverse is also true. When you discover somebody on LinkedIn who you wish to connect with and send them an invitation to do so, there is a high degree of likelihood that they will visit your profile (if they do not know you) as a part of their process in deciding whether or not to accept your invitation. If your profile is totally unprofessional (typos, incomplete, no photo or a less than professional one), you lose.

Your headline should provide people with some idea of who you are and what you do. Some people will put their title in this section, whereas others might list their key skills. Some others, including myself, have chosen to use this section to highlight what we do for others. Currently, my headline reads, "We show businesses how to leverage social sales tools, techniques, strategies, and Social CRM to increase their revenues!"

LinkedIn has its own powerful built-in search engine which we can use to find people who fit our target criteria, and those same people can use this engine to find vendors that fit their expressed needs. The secret is keywords. Think about what keywords people would use if they were looking for someone like you who offers your products and services. Enter these keywords into the LinkedIn advanced search, modify the search with your geographic area, and hit "search". LinkedIn will bring up member profiles that match these search parameters. Open and look at the top few profile results. LinkedIn will highlight in yellow where each of these keywords are found in that person's profile. Use these profiles as guidelines to edit and enter these keywords into your own profile as one way to help optimize it for search.

Your company should have a page on LinkedIn, and you should also keep this page updated with fresh information and articles/topics of interest. Encourage others to follow your page. Folks who do are voluntarily opting in to your messages. LinkedIn has recently introduced a new feature called Showcases for company pages that will allow LinkedIn users to follow news on your specific offerings that might be of interest to that user, while filtering out information on other products that may not be of interest.

For more information on setting up your LinkedIn personal profile and pages, a very good recent article by HubSpot titled *"The Ultimate Cheat Sheet for Mastering LinkedIn"* can be found in the appendix.

Twitter

Your profile has 160 characters with which you can tell your story; it also provides you with the ability to add your location, your photo, a page background, and a website. All Twitter users have *a handle* (@craigmjamieson) that is unique to them, but Twitter will also display your real name, should you choose to share it (I recommend that you do).

Twitter is the only network that does not offer a company page, at least not yet. However, there are services such as Rebel Mouse that will allow you to create a page that will aggregate everything you share on Twitter and will even automatically organize your updates by categories. These services could be used as a source for content that might be shared with the other networks and would direct people to that page to learn more about what you talk about on Twitter. This is another great way to establish your interests and expertise!

Facebook

While your profile on Facebook should include your business-related information, it is more about where you have lived and the things that you like, such as music, sports, reading, movies, and so on. It's personal. Once again, we have to remember that people will often buy from people when they feel that they have something in common. This may be something as simple as a shared love of gardening.

Company pages, originally called Fan Pages, are where businesses do business on Facebook. In fact, for some companies, their Facebook page serves as their storefront and/or website.

Google+

Profiles found on Google+ are very similar to those found on Facebook. With the introduction of Google+, what used to be your Google profile is now your plus profile. As a result of this, your profile will follow you around on all sites that are Google products.

Company pages are available on Google+.

Connecting with others

All of the networks will provide you with the ability to upload your existing e-mail lists to the service. From there, the service will identify the people you currently know who are already on the network, and you will be given an opportunity to connect or request to connect with those people. E-mail addresses are typically the glue that holds this process together.

What this also means is that while you may have somebody's business e-mail address, they may very well use a personal e-mail address for the social networks. Therefore, people you may wish to discover during this upload process might not be immediately identified.

When connecting with others, we have three business-specific goals. They are as follows:

> ➤ Connect with the right people
>
> ➤ Maximize the chances of our invitation to connect being accepted
>
> ➤ Once connected, develop that relationship

There are a few schools of thought regarding who you should connect with. From a purely business perspective, we would suggest that you will want to connect with the following people:

> ➤ Your customers and your prospective customers
>
> ➤ People who can refer you to customers
>
> ➤ Folks who you can share information with
>
> ➤ Thought leaders from your industry

These are relationships that can become or lead to revenues. On the other hand, you may be one of those people who wants to connect with anybody and everybody. That's all well and good, but it may be more effective for you to build relationships with hundreds of people who fit your target market profile than it will be with thousands who do not. Food for thought.

LinkedIn

LinkedIn employs a connection hierarchy. People who you are connected to directly are considered to be your first-degree connections. Those connected to your first-degree people become your second-degree connections, and then those connected to them become your third-degree connections.

Earlier, we talked about using LinkedIn advanced search in order to optimize our profiles so that prospective customers can easily find us. Now, we will use this same tool to find people that we will wish to potentially invite to connect. Think of keywords that meet your desired connection profiles, perform the search, and review your results.

There are two ways to send connection requests on LinkedIn. One is with a template invitation, *"Hi, I'd like to add you to my professional network on LinkedIn"*, and the second is with a personalized invitation. Whenever possible, **always send a personalized invitation** and make sure that this invitation will provide that person with a good reason to accept it. Sending a personalized invitation will not always be possible if LinkedIn suspects that you may already know this person. Your best way to maximize the chances of customizing your invitation is to send it from that person's profile page. We would suggest that you **IGNORE** all LinkedIn suggestions to connect with people when that suggestion offers you a one-click invite to connect, as these may subvert your ability to write a personalized invitation.

In certain cases, LinkedIn does offer a less formal connection format. For example, you can follow someone who is in a shared group with you. Following somebody means that their updates, as it pertains to that group, will appear in your news stream. You can also follow companies and influencers (as determined by LinkedIn) and have those/their updates appear in your news stream.

Twitter

Connecting with people on Twitter is a very simple process. You choose to *follow* them, which is to say that you want to view their updates in your news stream. The user will be notified that you have followed them and then they can choose to either follow you back (add your updates to their news stream) or to not follow you back. They also have an option to block you, but this is rarely done, unless you turn out to be a spammer or a trash talker; so, don't be either. When you follow somebody, you have also granted them the permission to private message you. If they do not follow you back, you do not have the privilege to private message them. Private messages, or DMs (direct messages), are visible to the two parties only.

As with LinkedIn, you will wish to target the people who you wish to follow on Twitter. Examples of targeting would include by location, occupation, or skill set. This can be done via Twitter's standard or advanced search or with one of the dozens of free and paid applications that will help you narrow and identify your search.

Using Twitter's advanced search, you can also search Twitter updates for mentions of specific phrases or keywords, and you can also narrow these responses down by basic sentiments (positive, negative, question). You might look for, for example, mentions of your brand, people who are expressing frustration with a competitor, or folks who are asking questions such as "Does anybody have any recommendations for good (your service or product) in the Boise area?" These would be great examples of people who may need your services! Searches, once configured to your liking, can also be saved for future use.

Hash tags are another way to conduct searches on Twitter, and they are also used to draw attention to individual tweets. For example, I could create a hash tag for this book such as #socialcrmbook and then ask people to use this hash tag when talking about the book. Anybody would then be able to click on this hash tag on any individual update, and all tweets using the same hash tag would be displayed.

Facebook

You don't connect on Facebook, you become *friends*. Facebook also provides you with the ability to search for people by name or by keywords, and Facebook graph search provides some other interesting and powerful ways to search (including for photos, friends, music, and restaurants) by anticipating and suggesting your search parameters.

Search can be used, for example, to find companies and/or people who work at specific (target) companies. Alternatively, you would be able to conduct a search for people in your target market by just typing in "Find people who are X", with "X" being a title or an industry, for example, "Find people who are architects".

Facebook pages offer another, albeit different, connection level. When somebody *likes* your page, they have opted into the messages that you share on your page. While getting likes is important, it is what you do with these in terms of engagement and conversions (they become paying customers) that matters more.

Google+

Much like Twitter, people elect to follow you on Google+, and you are then given the opportunity to follow them back. However, when you do elect to do this, Google+ asks you to do so by assigning them to one or more *circles*. Circles are a way for you to keep your connections on Google+ organized. For example, you may have one circle for customers, another for friends, and still another for vendors. Companies found on Google+ are treated in the same manner as are people. You add them to a circle. You may wish to have separate circles for people and companies or to group them together. Google+ does offer advanced search features that will allow you to target people who you may wish to follow, and search also has the ability to discover keywords in updates that have been shared, for example, brand mentions or an expressed need for a product or a service.

Share updates and engage

You **must** be willing to engage (converse) with others on the social channels in exactly the same manner in which you must be willing to do this in real life! In business, we suggest a system of progressive engagement that we call *taps* and *touches*. Examples of taps would be liking someone's update or sharing that update to your own network. A touch would be more direct and personal such as leaving a comment or sending them a private message. Taps and touches lead to formal connections and more personal direct engagement that is, they lead to building relationships.

LinkedIn

While not as conversational as, say, Facebook, LinkedIn does allow you to share updates that your network may find of interest. It also allows you to engage with others by commenting, liking, or by sharing their updates with your network. Any update shared can be brought to the attention of somebody (like a Twitter @message) by just starting to type their name and then selecting them from a drop-down list. Engagement is the beginning of every relationship. It is conversation with and learning more about each other. Therefore, engagement is your priority.

Sharing updates helps establish your expertise and encourages others to engage and connect with you. You will want a percentage of your updates to reflect your industry and to establish you as being the expert in that industry. Your focus should be on education rather than on selling. If you are a value-added reseller of I.T. services, share articles with others that provide tips to buy and utilize these types of services. While you are not selling your services, you will be positioning yourself as the go-to person if such needs arise.

When entering any conversation, and this holds true regardless of the social channel, it is critical that you first listen and then decide if you have anything of value to contribute, and only at the appropriate time do you enter the conversation and only with the appropriate message.

You do have the ability to share links that can be to articles, videos, and just about anything, and LinkedIn recently added the ability to upload and share documents (.pdf, .doc, and so on).

Twitter

There are a number of ways to engage with others on Twitter. They are as follows:

> **Reply**: This is also called a mention or an @message. When you add somebody's Twitter handle to the message (@craigmjamieson), while this message will be public, it will also be brought directly to that person's attention.

> **Retweet**: The act of retweeting (RT) is when you forward somebody's message on to your followers. This will earn you immediate points within the Twitter community.

> **Favorite**: When you favorite somebody's tweet, they will be notified of this. This act is like marking something as "read for later".

> **Direct message** (**DM**): This is a private message on Twitter between two parties.

> **Hash tags**: This is a method on Twitter to tag updates for easy search. Examples of their use can be found in this chapter.

Twitter can be very powerful to find new people and new opportunities through search. It is also a very well-recognized customer service platform, and there are many applications, including some SCRMs, that have integrated Twitter strictly for this purpose. Here is a customer-service story for you.

Some years ago, when I was just becoming active on Twitter, I ran into an issue with my computer's antivirus software. This application had determined that the absolute best way to ensure that I did not contract a virus was to not allow me to get on the Internet ... AT ALL! Obviously, this was a problem. I went to my laptop and e-mailed support. No response. I got on the phone and called support. The same result. Finally, in a fit of frustration, I called them out on Twitter and did so by name. Minutes later, I received an @ message from their support department that almost begged me to be of assistance. Hmmm. Somebody is listening and responding. This is commonly known as *brand monitoring*.

The lesson is that if you say to yourself "I'm not on social media," the real answer may be "You are on social media, but you just don't know about it." Good news travels faster than almost anything except bad news.

Facebook

Facebook is very conversational (likes, comments, shares to my network), and it is also very visual. Make frequent use of images and videos, as these are guaranteed to attract attention and engagement. You can bring updates directly to the attention of another friend by simply typing in their name and then choosing them from the auto-suggest drop-down list.

Google+

Google+ is very similar to Facebook in terms of engaging. In place of likes, Google+ offers *+1's*. Any update can be directed to individuals by simply preceding their name with a "+" and then selecting them from the auto-suggest drop-down list that will appear as you type.

While the style of sharing is very similar to Facebook, the community itself tends to be quite different. Those who are active on Google+ tend to be a more early-adopter and a tech-oriented bunch. Some people have been known to refer to Google+ as "Facebook with a tie". Hangouts are eight-way video chats that can also be publicly broadcasted and that offer a truly unique way to engage with others on the network.

Finally, being a part of Google, there is very tight integration with all of Google's products; so, for example, videos that you upload to YouTube can be automatically shared to Google+. This same rule holds true with images that you store on Picasa. Just about every Google product is in some way connected with Google+, including Gmail, Calendar, and Drive (which includes Docs, Sheets, Presentations, and Forms).

Focus with lists and circles

Let's be honest. If you are already active with social networking, your current connections are likely a fairly eclectic bunch. Using Facebook as an example, you may be friends with relatives, neighbors, customers, acquaintances, people you went to school with, and people who you just find to be interesting or who maybe make you laugh. As a business, this presents some challenges as it makes it very difficult for us to **focus** on the following three key areas:

1. We would like to be able to group our customers by a number of factors. This may be geographically or by industry type, for example.

2. We want to be listening to what our customers and prospective customers are talking about without being distracted by what everyone else has to say.

3. We need to be able to share business-related content with business people, not with our friends and vice versa.

This is where lists and circles become invaluable. They allow you to focus on both key areas: listening and sharing.

LinkedIn

At this time, LinkedIn does not offer a way to focus on updates from a group of selected connections. However, LinkedIn will allow you to group your connections together by way of *tags*. You can create multiple tags, and each connection can also be assigned to more than one tag. For example, you may have a tag for prospects. From LinkedIn's *Contacts* tab, you would then be able to view all of your contacts that you have tagged as being prospects and then formulate a targeted approach from there. This can include a template private message to be sent to everybody who matches a particular tag.

LinkedIn's contact database not only includes people who you are connected to on LinkedIn, it also includes people from your address book, and your Facebook friends. Any of these can be tagged.

Twitter

The biggest single challenge with Twitter is that there is just so much of it. Following maybe thousands of people means that you have thousands of people sharing updates, all at the same time, and all of these are flowing simultaneously into your newsfeed. How can you cut through the noise and get directly to those updates that are most important to you? The solution is *lists*.

Twitter provides you with the ability to create public or private lists (more on this in a minute) and then add people that you follow to one or more of these lists. Some examples of lists that you may wish to create would be as follows:

➤ Customers

➤ Suspects

➤ Prospects

➤ Referrers

➤ Vendors

➤ Team members

➤ Brand advocates

➤ Influencers and industry leaders

➤ Competitors

Now, if you wish to see just what your customers are talking about on Twitter, you call up that list and all other tweets are filtered out. Private lists are for your eyes only. Public lists are discoverable by others. More so, public lists can also be followed by others; there is a difference between following an individual and following a list. When you follow a list, updates from the people on this list will appear on your newsfeed, but you have not formally followed these individuals, and they have no idea that you are even following their updates. Therefore, if you are looking for a follow back, you will want to follow them directly.

Would I want to keep my best customers on a public list? Probably not. This is not a list that I would want a competitor to find and follow. On the other hand, if my competitor created a list of their best customers and made it public, would I want to follow that? You bet I would!

Facebook

Facebook does allow you to group your friends into *lists*. While Facebook calls everybody a friend, we will create lists for friends, customers, prospective customers, vendors, and any business-related category that you may wish to have the ability to focus on. Facebook will also create some *smart lists* for you. Typical smart lists include people who went to the same high school as you, those who went to the same college as you, and people who you work with. Creating lists on Facebook provides you with two important benefits. They are as follows:

> ➤ You can filter your news stream to only show updates from people who are on a particular list
> ➤ You can share a specific update only with people who are on a specific list

This means that not only can you focus on what is being discussed by specific groups (customers), but you can share your business-related updates only with people who will value them (not your extended family members).

Google+

Very much like Facebook, Google+ will allow you to filter your news stream to show only updates from a specific circle, and when you share an update, it can be directed to specific circles, people, or even e-mailed directly to specific people who you have in your circle. Once again, you will want to create circles for the same groups of people who we mentioned earlier when referring to Twitter (business circles), and people can belong to more than one circle. For example, a customer who is also in manufacturing might belong to our "Customers" circle as well as our "Manufacturing" circle.

Groups and events

In general, *you will want to be involved with groups that are frequented by your target market.* For example, my areas of specialty are social sales and Social CRM, and I run a group on LinkedIn called "Boise B2B Sales and Marketing Professionals". What does the membership look like? It looks like my target market. You will be able to join the existing groups or consider starting one on your own that will best meet your needs. If you have a business-related event that you wish to promote, you will want to take advantage of the social networks to help you with this!

LinkedIn

LinkedIn groups are where like-minded people huddle up and share some serious conversation. There are groups for alumni, employers, industries, and more. You can belong to up to 50 groups, but we would suggest that you join no more than 10 that **you can be active on.** The cream floats to the top, and people who are active on groups gain the greatest visibility within that group. Visibility = Business Opportunity.

While some groups are private (by invitation only), most are now public. However, requests to join these groups may still be moderated. What groups will you want to belong to? How about groups where your target market tends to be active? This holds true for any social network that offers a groups feature. Fish like to school up, and we would suggest that your best fishing will be in these ponds. As someone who spent a large percentage of his latter career in the electric sign industry, my best referrers were commercial real estate, developers, architects, and the trades. There are many groups for each of these.

The beauty of LinkedIn groups is that they are *connection agnostic*. This means that you do not need to establish first-degree, second-degree, or even third-degree connections with anyone in order to be in the same group and then be able to converse and engage with any other group member. Outstanding! Active group members gain visibility, and if you are providing valuable information to your target market, who will they call when they need to avail themselves of services that you are able to provide? Likely, the answer will be "you".

LinkedIn no longer has an events application. However, you can create events on other networks such as Facebook or Google+ or use a service such as EventBrite and then share those events on LinkedIn by including the link to the event in your update.

Twitter

Twitter does not offer groups, per se. However, you can organize and participate in what are called *Tweetchats*. Twitter updates often include the use of *hash tags*, and these are actually search links. You can then filter updates to show only those that include a specific hash tag. Quite often, people will organize these group chats by creating a hash tag that all participants can then use to follow along and engage in the conversation, for example, #socialcrm.

You might offer a Tweetchat (not an officially supported Twitter application) for customers where you discuss best uses for your product or service. Keep in mind that Tweetchats are public, meaning that anyone can listen in; therefore, you will wish to avoid sharing confidential information. However, if you are showing your customers, in a public forum, how they might use your products better, others will notice, and these same people may be searching for a vendor just like you!

Events that appear on Twitter have been created elsewhere (EventBrite, Evite, or on another network such as Facebook or Google+) and are shared by the use of a link.

Facebook

Facebook groups are quite popular and can be either private or public. As with LinkedIn, you will want to join groups that are frequented by people who have the potential of doing business with you.

Facebook also has a very strong events application that allows you to invite others and track registrations and RSVPs. You can advertise and market any business-related event on Facebook, including events that are free and that are fee based. For example, you might promote a workshop, an open house, a business show, a charity event, or a product introduction. Events might also be virtual, such as a webinar, a live feed from a show, or a closed circuit broadcast.

Google+

As opposed to groups, Google+ allows you to create and join *communities*. The same business-focused rules for LinkedIn and Facebook apply to Google+; go where your market is and be active and visible! Groups and communities are the absolute best places to establish your expertise with those who will need and appreciate it!

Google+ also has a very nice events application (similar to Facebook and with the same business-related applications), and these events can include inviting people to attend a private or public hangout (eight-way video chat) and/or a broadcasted hangout. Maybe you would like to use a hangout to invite a customer to meet with your product development team, or if you are in a certain phase of a project for them, you might want to have a meeting with the customer and the department heads who are involved. A broadcasted hangout could be a live feed from a new product introduction. These events can also be added automatically to your Google calendar.

Summary

In this chapter, we defined *Social Business* as the business-related application of social media. Being a social business, in essence, means that we will take those practices that we already excel at in real life, and we will then utilize the social networks and Social CRM to leverage these in our quest to consistently exceed our customers' expectations. Here are the key points to take away from this chapter:

> Strategies employed by a social business are both external (customer facing) and internal (company facing), and it is critical that all company departments work in concert to meet company goals, particularly as they pertain to our level of customer satisfaction.

> The social networks themselves (LinkedIn, Twitter, Facebook, Google+, and so on) are some of the vehicles that we will be able to use to discover new relationships and opportunities and continue to nurture both. Social networking augments, rather than replaces, our traditional sales, marketing, and customer-service activities.

➤ In order to be successful with social networking and social business, you must be willing to engage (converse) with others on the social networks. This is how relationships first begin and then continue to grow.

➤ You should not just connect with people on the networks for the purpose of connecting. You need to rather connect **with a purpose** to the right people.

➤ Social networking will result in increased revenues as you turn relationships into convertible opportunities.

In our next chapter, we will explore the ways in which we can put these social channels and your activities on them to work for the purpose of generating new revenues and exceeding customer expectations. You will be shown the roles that Social CRM will play in achieving these goals.

3

Laying the Groundwork for Social CRM

By this point, you should have a solid fundamental understanding of Social Business and how Social CRM (SCRM) will allow you to manage and leverage these fantastic new opportunities! This chapter will describe the first steps that you will want to take prior to choosing your SCRM, let alone thinking about implementing it. In fact, these steps will help ensure the right choice of a Social CRM, its successful implementation, and your business being able to realize the long-term benefits of this system.

We will discuss how to do the following:

- ➤ Assess your Social Business status
- ➤ Identify who in your business should be using Social CRM
- ➤ Choose who will take the lead on this initiative
- ➤ Discover those networks frequented by your customers
- ➤ Get buy-ins from your users

Each of these is a critical step in the process, and skipping steps will likely result in a negative experience for you, your people, and your company; so, don't skip steps!

Assess your social business status

Soon, we will begin the process of defining your needs as it relates to Social CRM. A large part of this will be contingent on first ensuring that your company and your people have established the necessary presences on the social channels themselves. It is time to take an inventory of your current status pertaining to this topic. Here are some questions that you should be asking yourself as well as of your team members:

➤ Who in your company is currently active on the social networks, and which channels are they active on (individually)?

➤ To what level are they active, and how comfortable are they on each of the networks that they currently use? How can we help them be better?

➤ What networks should they add and what help will we need to provide them in maximizing their presence on each?

➤ As a company, have we established pages on LinkedIn, Facebook, and Google+ (dependent on where our company needs to be active)?

➤ If not, what do we need to do to establish these pages and who will do that?

➤ How about our sources for content? Do we have a blog, channels on YouTube and SlideShare, or other web-based presences? If not, do we need them and who will get those set up?

Tip

Make a list of each action that will need to be taken, and formulate a plan to ensure its completion. Do this by person as well as for your company.

Who in your business should be using Social CRM?

Traditionally, CRM systems have been most widely used by sales and marketing people with probably an emphasis on salespeople. Certainly, the same people will want to have SCRM in their business tool kit. However, whereas traditional CRM is more of a database with little to no interaction with your customers, SCRM is **ALL** about interaction with existing and prospective customers!

Furthermore, it is about interfacing with the other team members within your company, and make no mistake; people who work for your organization may be employees, but they are first and foremost your customer-satisfaction team! With this in mind, just about anybody within your organization can make good use of SCRM!

As a basic rule of thumb, if you have somebody who is expected to interact with a customer or a prospective customer, or if you have staff that work together with the common goal of exceeding customer expectations, then these people need to be connected together on your SCRM if you wish to maximize its effectiveness. You are a team, and many SCRMs will allow you to collaborate, online, as a team. These departments would naturally include sales, marketing, customer service, and design. Also, don't forget to include your management and support personnel!

The following table will identify some of the most common SCRM uses by department:

	Marketing	Sales	Customer Service	Product Design	Collaboration
Gain Insights	Brand-tracking,research communities	Identifying customer grievances	Identifying problems	Identifying trends and ideas	Profiles, groups, and activity streams
Create Activities	Changing the medium or the message	Converting leads	Solving problems	Acknowledging ideas	Shared workspaces
Content and Campaigns	Viral marketing campaigns	Referral campaigns	Suggestion campaigns	Suggestion campaigns	Blogs and Wikis
Communities	Advocate communities	Advocate communities	Self-service communities	Idea communities	Employee and partner communities

Make a note

The preceding table has been adapted from `http://slideshare.net/jeremiah_owyang/social-crm-the-new-rules-of-relationship-management`.

As you can see, we have identified four company departments (marketing, sales, customer service, and product design) along with a fifth general area of collaboration, which can be internal (within your company), external (with those who are outside of your company), or both. Each department, with the help of SCRM, can also do the following:

➤ **Gain Insights**: Gather information pertaining to their particular department's responsibilities by targeted monitoring and engaging on the social channels. This information can then be used to plan needed activities.

➤ **Create Activities**: Activities are generally initiated as a result of the "insight-gathering" process. In this sense, we are reacting to an identified need.

➤ **Initiate Content and Campaigns**: Based on the information that we have gathered, we are now able to develop marketing and other campaigns that address the identified needs or our target market.

➤ **Engage in Communities**: Online communities are very much like groups that will encourage discussion among their members and can also be leveraged to amplify your messages. When somebody feels as though they are a part of a community (your business), they will naturally adopt the behaviors that are associated with actually being a part of your business.

Your company, any company, will always be stronger when they work together to satisfy the needs of their customers. Having your customer know that there is a team behind each individual, one that is dedicated to them, creates a much stronger bond than will isolate them from the rest of your people.

Tip

Make a preliminary list of people within your organization who will be candidates for using your SCRM, and diagram their relationship to each other as well as to your customers and prospective customers.

Who will take the lead?

Somebody needs to take this bull by the horns. While we are not talking about General George S. Patton, you will want and require a leader. Your ideal person will be one who leads by consensus and not by conflict. Being a small business, having this responsibility shared by a committee is probably not necessary, although having representation (at the appropriate time) from your various departments would be recommended. Still, somebody does need to be the go-to person who will follow up and follow through and hold others accountable when necessary. We need to keep this train on its tracks. Suggested qualities for this person include the following:

> Detail-oriented

> Persuasive

> A good listener who displays empathy

> Well organized

> Action driven

> Having a strong moderator skill set

Suggestions for your meeting

You will want to sit down with this individual(s) and have very detailed discussions regarding your overall vision and their role in presenting that to your team. Discuss with them why you are considering this investment and what your expectations (of your team and of the company) will be, that is, short, medium, and long term. This person will be your partner in this process, so having an open and honest dialogue is a must. Encourage them to poke whatever holes that they might find in your reasoning and future plans.

On that subject, if this person is not yourself (the owner), you will want to make sure that everyone within your organization is aware that this individual is your choice to head up this initiative, that they have your full support, and that they will be speaking as you in this matter.

The same person may be in charge of forming an eventual team. While you may be the one who is providing the push and your lead person is the one who is taking charge, you may eventually require a system administrator who will be tasked with the day-to-day operation of the system, as well as one or more strong trainers who will assist in making sure that the users' needs are being met.

Taking the lead should not be confused with ownership of the initiative itself. Ownership implies that this aspect of the business belongs to one single department or individual. This is commonly referred to as *silo thinking*. Examples of silos would be the not-so-uncommon occurrence where sales, marketing, customer service, and IT are in a continuing discussion over who should own SCRM. The answer is nobody and everybody. As a team that is dedicated to exceeding customer expectations, this is a shared responsibility, and silo thinking has a very strong potential to damage your overall goals.

Tip

Choose your lead person(s) for your SCRM project, and schedule your first meeting with them to discuss the steps in this process.

Where are my customers?

If you are still thinking, *"My customers are not using social media, so what use would any of this be for me?"*, then think again. This is likely more a conjecture than it is fact. Even if this were true, does this mean that your customers will never use social media? Perhaps, but not very likely. The simple truth is that social media is becoming increasingly more accepted for small business. Two of the reasons for this are accessibility (including mobile applications) as well as dramatic improvements in ease of use.

I asked myself the same question 6 years ago and decided to upload all of my existing contacts to each social network, prior to committing, just to find out for myself how many of my connections were currently using social media. The results were incredibly disheartening! Maybe 5 percent of my existing customers were using LinkedIn, and the results for the other networks went downhill from there. I struggled with the decision to even proceed and invest the time that would be needed in a pursuit which, on the surface, displayed little to no chance of my ever realizing any sort of return.

What I failed to realize at the time was that I needed to be able to expand my network beyond those people who I already knew and worked with. I desperately needed to know those people who my connections knew and I did not. Even if you are limited geographically, this makes no difference! If you can answer yes to any of the following questions, your existing network still has tremendous growth potential!

1. Do I have any competitors who are still in business?
2. Are there any accounts that I would like to penetrate but have not been able to?
3. Are there any businesses in my own territory that I do not know as well as I should?

4. Do my existing customers have the ability to buy more from me?

5. Would I like to see my existing customers more willingly refer me to others who might need our services?

Grow your network and grow your business!

There are many sources that are available to you which will help you determine the networks that your customers (target and existing) are frequenting:

➤ Your SCRM may have the capability to mine your contacts for their social profile information. If not, there are some third-party e-mail add-ons that have this social discovery capability, as do the standard search engines (Google, Bing, Yahoo).

➤ Search for both individuals and companies on the networks themselves. For example, having a company presence on LinkedIn will also show you employees of that company who are also on LinkedIn.

➤ Visit their company websites and look for social network icons that will allow you to connect with the company. Such icons can generally be found on the website's home page.

➤ Ask them. When all else fails, ask your customers if they are active on the social networks, and if so, which ones. This would also be a good time to ask them how they would prefer to be contacted by you. You might be amazed. Their answers will range from phone to e-mail to text to Twitter and so on.

We would also suggest that, at least starting out, you limit your focus to what are currently the four largest networks—LinkedIn, Facebook, Google+, and Twitter—as these have the widest adoption rate and, therefore, will represent the greatest opportunity to reach your target market.

However, once again, you will want to concentrate your efforts on those channels that are frequented by your customers and your prospective customers, and these might include services such as Instagram or Pinterest, or there may also be large networks that are very popular in certain countries, such as QQ, Weibo, Kontakte, Renren, and so on.

Tip

Start researching which social networks your customers and your prospective customers are already active on.

Getting buy-ins from your users

It's great to be "The General", but this is only as good as having your troops behind you who are willing, able, and ready to go into battle. Selecting and implementing your Social CRM is no different. All personnel that will be involved in this process need to be invested in and excited about seeing it to its successful conclusion!

Never request buy-ins

Let's start by saying this. The absolute worst way to get buy-ins from your users is to announce that you have invested in a SCRM and that you want everybody to be supportive of **your decision**. At this time, we are not asking your team for buy-ins on a specific product or solution. What we do want is a buy-in to discussing the concept itself. Which of these two statements is likely to resonate more positively with your team members?

"We would like to talk to you about implementing Social CRM"

"We would like to talk to you about exploring some ways to make our company more effective in finding and servicing our customers"

Bring your people in very early in the process and place them in an ownership position in all phases of the discussion, choices, and development. As they will be the ones using the tool on a daily basis, it only makes good sense to ask for their input before, instead of after. Stress on the point that they are critical elements and that you need them to be involved in this project going forward.

Although, we are now discussing the concept, and the actual needs of the system will be determined later, you need to best be prepared for concerns that will be raised. In fact, you should encourage and welcome these. It is far better to find out now than it is to try to address these later on in the project and only after a substantial investment of, perhaps, both time and money! Anticipating concerns also provides us with the flexibility to bring these up ourselves in order to promote the discussion. Some of these may be as follows:

➤ *"Who is going to use this?"*

➤ *"When are we planning on doing this?"*

➤ *"That won't work because ... "*

➤ *"What does I.T. think of this?"*

➤ *"How do you envision "x" working with this new system?"*

➤ *"Can we afford this?"*

➤ *"How are we supposed to make the time available to get this done?"*

➤ *"Have you thought of ...?"*

Ultimately, we are invited into a conversation and allowed to do the following:

> ➤ Ask questions
> ➤ Freely express our views
> ➤ Provide input

At this point, we need to know that we are being listened to and, in turn, regardless of the eventual outcome, we will have assumed a sense of ownership in the process. Ownership, in this sense, is good. As owners, we all have a vested interest in its success.

Addressing salesperson hesitancy

I have spent my entire career as either a salesperson, a sales manager, or as a business owner, and from experience, I can tell you that salespeople have traditionally resisted CRM initiatives. Their perception is that a CRM implementation (and SCRM will be no different) will be:

> ➤ Time consuming and that time will be taken away from their available selling hours
> ➤ A frustrating new learning experience
> ➤ Will force them into areas that they are not comfortable with (paperwork)
> ➤ That CRM is just another way for management to keep their foot on the back of a salesperson's neck

What do we know about salespeople? Salespeople are motivated (and this is not limited to only these items) by money, competition, praise, and winning new accounts. This is easy to appreciate as, simply put, most salespeople are paid to sell. Still, it is not uncommon for them to possess traits that will drive most managers to the precipice of a nervous breakdown.

They are also known for hating paperwork, being notoriously disorganized, and chafing at authority. Even if considered to be employees, they will view themselves to be independent contractors who are not subject to the same rules and expectations that are placed on other staff members.

When we understand (and anticipate) common reasons for salesperson hesitancy and combine these with an appreciation of their motivations, goals, and personality proclivities, answering their concerns becomes a much easier process. The keys will be to focus on these and to answer each in an honest and straightforward manner.

Let's take a look at some of the following common objections:

Concern: *"Who came up with this idea and why was it not discussed with me first?"* Don't get this one wrong. Your answer will determine whether or not this will be a constructive conversation or one that will be contentious.

Answer: This is very early in the process and no decisions have been made. In fact, we are discussing this with you first before we take any further action, and your feedback will be invaluable!

Concern: *"Why do you want me to do this?"* Salespeople and sales managers may have different agendas. In the salesperson's mind, if they are at or above quota, why is there a need to change anything? If it isn't broken, then why are we fixing it?

Answer: The answer to this concern is that you want to help them increase their earnings and make their work less time consuming, more efficient, and more rewarding.

Concern: *"What are you planning to do with this information?"* Many salespeople are hesitant to share what they may view as being their proprietary information. Of course, they work for you, and this information belongs to your business; however, this does not change their perception of this matter.

Answer: We want to help you understand what you will want to do in order to achieve your goals. The information generated will also help us pinpoint those areas where we can best support your efforts.

Concern: *"I don't have time to do frivolous paperwork and should only be judged on my performance."* This is totally understandable as the time used doing paperwork is time not being spent selling and making commissions.

Answer: This will actually minimize all paperwork, and much of what you are now doing when you come back to the office, you will be able to do out in the field!

Concern: *"How will this help me sell more?"*

Answer: Having the ability to sell more is perhaps the most important key element in changing salesperson attitudes toward SCRM. Selling has always been about building relationships, and *relationships* have never been a part of a traditional CRM despite including that term in the name. If they have had a negative experience with CRM, stress on the point that SCRM is an entirely different animal and one that has been designed to help them sell more, not less!

What salespeople want and can SCRM actually deliver it?

> *They want to sell more product or services.* Used properly, SCRM has the potential to dramatically increase sales from both your existing customers as well as your prospective ones.

> *They want to build closer relationships with their customers.* Relationships are social, and this is where SCRM excels. Your salespeople will be able to discover common areas of interest as well as common connections and will be able to more fully understand and appreciate the needs of their clients like they have never been able to do so before.

> ➤ *They wish to be viewed as being professionals.* Professionals demonstrate professional habits and ensure that their expertise is recognized by others. We all want to be perceived as being the experts in our given fields, and social networking is a unique and effective way to accomplish these goals.

> ➤ *They want more referrals.* When you consistently exceed customer expectations, referrals naturally follow! Social CRM will assist you in becoming memorable and remarkable in the eyes of your customers.

> ➤ *They want to be better organized:* Nobody can operate effectively with sticky notes all over their desk and random notes falling out of client folders.

> ➤ *They want easy access to customer information at any time.* Your customers are mobile and so are your salespeople. Having important customer information at their fingertips, any place and any time, is a critical contributing element to success.

> ➤ *They want to be able to accurately forecast their sales (commission checks) and to smooth out the peak and valley payday rollercoaster.* It is very difficult to project your earnings if you have no accurate way to track your opportunities and then to monitor and adjust their status.

> ➤ *They want more time for selling and to spend less time on paperwork.* SCRM, particularly when combined with mobile, will generate more productive selling hours out of every working day.

The answer to each of these is a resounding "yes"!

Later on, and this holds true for all personnel who will be utilizing the system, we will discuss the necessary steps to ensure that they will continue to employ the system consistently and effectively.

Tip

Sit down with your key person and discuss and strategize your approach to your other team members. Anticipate and prepare for potential objections to your project. Schedule and hold your team meetings.

Summary

In this chapter, we discussed how important it is to lay the correct groundwork, the foundation so to speak, within your business prior to actively beginning the process of selecting and then implementing your Social CRM. Let's recap the important points:

> ➤ It will be very difficult to determine how we are going to get to "point B" without first determining our current location on the map. Take an inventory, and do this for every individual who will be using your Social CRM as well as for your company, of the present status of your representation on the social channels that you will be utilizing. After completing this list, create a plan to fortify your weak areas and fill in your coverage gaps.

> Company personnel who interact with customers as well as those who interact with each other in the direct pursuit of exceeding customer expectations are excellent candidates to be SCRM users. Make a preliminary list of people within your organization who will be candidates to use your SCRM and diagram their relationship to each other as well as to your customers and prospective customers.

> This may ultimately involve one or more persons, depending on the size and complexity of your business, but somebody needs to be placed in a position of being in charge. This person(s) will take your vision forward to the other members of your company who will be instrumental in ensuring that your SCRM project will get off on the right foot and will also be completed successfully. Choose your lead person(s) for your SCRM project and schedule your first meeting with them to discuss the steps in this process

> You will want to concentrate your social networking activities on those networks that are already frequented by your customers and your prospective customers. **Do not** assume that your target market is not using social media. Do the research needed to make an informed evaluation. Start researching which social networks your customers and your prospective customers are already active on.

> Getting buy-ins from your users will make or break your project. Not having buy-ins from users is probably the single most common reason given for failed SCRM projects. Sit down with your key person and discuss and strategize your approach to your other team members. Anticipate and prepare for potential objections to your project. Schedule and hold your team meetings.

In our next chapter, we will be discussing in great detail the steps that you will want to take in order to correctly assess and define your Social CRM needs, prior to making any investment in a solution. This will be a critical chapter, in that it will help ensure that you will choose the right product for your small business needs.

Define Your Social CRM Needs Prior to Any Investment

Understanding your small business needs today and anticipating your future needs will be critical elements in choosing which SCRM will be right for your small business. Without a clear vision of the features that you will require and how you plan to use your SCRM, choosing the right platform will be difficult at best. In this chapter, you will learn to do the following:

- ➤ Set goals and expectations
- ➤ Document and prioritize your needs
- ➤ Plan for a mobile SCRM
- ➤ Recap your needs by developing a matrix

By this point, you have ideally selected your key person to head up this initiative, and you have also presented the overall concept of SCRM to your team members. As we go through this chapter, it will be important to gain feedback from all departments and personnel who will be involved in implementing and/or using your SCRM. As they will be the ones who will be using it on a daily basis, this is a good business practice.

In order for an SCRM system to make any sense at all, you and your people must have made the decision and commitment to become a social business. This means that you must be willing to be active and to engage with your clients and prospective clients on the social networks. Additionally, you'll have determined that being a social business is the right strategic move for your small business based on your target market. Without these pledges, you might wish to consider whether a CRM (which does not incorporate social networking) or SCRM (which does) is right for you.

At the end of this chapter, you should have a good solid vision of what your SCRM will need to include. You will then be in a good position to compare your needs' matrix to SCRMs that are available, and accordingly, you will select the best possible choice for your needs.

Setting goals and expectations

Quite likely, you are experiencing certain pain points—areas you feel that your company could improve upon—and these may be the catalyst for your interest in SCRM as a potential solution for these needs. Setting goals that will address these areas, documenting the steps that you will take to achieve them by writing each down, and then deciding how you will be able to determine whether each goal has been achieved are all key elements to successful goal setting. Of course, the most important element is action. Don't talk. Do.

For example, your sales manager may wish to ensure that all leads are being followed up on, that closing ratios are increased, that current customers are being called on with the necessary frequency, and that salespeople maintain an adequate activity level of prospecting. Your marketing and customer support staff and management will often have similar goals specific to their departments.

In regard to your expectations, some may be reasonable, while others might prove to be unreasonable. The only way you will determine this is to think big and then find out whether or not your aspirations are attainable. You may find that while some of the SCRM features that you wish for are available, they may be out of your price range. Alternatively, while you are able to secure the needed feature "A", you will be forced to give up the nice features "C" and "F" in order to secure it.

Being willing to accept that there may be trade-offs is a reasonable expectation. Expecting to find the perfect SCRM, the one that meets all of your criteria, is probably an unreasonable expectation. However, SCRM is a rapidly moving target, and new innovations are being introduced practically daily.

This being said, after completing your evaluations, you may feel that you need to wait. You may be caught in the line of thinking that goes, "Someday the perfect system will be available and I will make my move at that time." While this may be all well and good, are you willing to give up the benefits that can be secured today, tangible results (think revenues) that you will never be able to recover, in order to wait for that perfect system? I would hope not.

Document and prioritize your needs

By now, you should have a clear general understanding of the benefits that are associated with SCRM, so let's now discuss specific features and functions that you will be looking for in a system.

As we go through each function, mark each with one of these three ratings:

> **Need**: This would be a must-have item in your new SCRM.

> **Nice**: While this is not an absolute necessity, it would be nice to have. It may be needed later.

> **Not needed**: There is no way that we need or will ever need this feature. It does not apply to our small business.

We will also divide this section by department: *general company needs, sales needs, marketing needs,* and *customer service needs.* We'll then further subdivide by management and staff. Both management and staff may have similar needs. However, one of the fundamental goals of every manager is to evaluate the efforts and initiatives that are relevant to their departments for their effectiveness, and then to have the option to adjust as required to increase their effectiveness. SCRM has the potential to provide your small business with the necessary information in order to do just that!

Typical SCRM configurations

SCRMs are typically organized into modules, which is one way to group records that are related to each other. For example, a Sales module may include multiple record types, which are as follows:

> - A contact record (person) will have that individual's contact information such as their names, e-mails, and so on

> - An account record (company) will contain the company website, headquarters' address, and so on

> - Deal records, which contain information that is unique to that specific opportunity

Your Customer Service module might have records for individual support cases and Marketing may have record types that correlate to campaigns.

Within each record itself, you will also likely find subsections for specific datasets that are associated with this record. Examples might be tasks and activities, notes, meetings, or individual opportunities.

All of these modules and individual records will typically be connected in some manner. For example, an opportunity will be linked to the person who makes the decision regarding that opportunity and that person will, in turn, be linked to the company that they work for.

General company needs – technical

General company needs will address fundamental questions that will impact your overall system choice and implementation. Technical specifications are primarily related to the nuts-and-bolts aspects of your SCRM, such as quantity limitations and technical requirements.

Number of users and storage requirements

The first question that you will need to answer is whether you will require a single-user or a multi-user system, and please think about your potential and/or planned growth before you answer that. Cloud-based systems that you will access via the Internet may be based on a per-user basis, or they may offer different levels for teams. For example, "X" dollars per month for up to five users and "Y" dollars per month for up to 10 users. You may be allowed to add users for an additional monthly fee per user.

Storage of your data (records, emails, documents, and so on) may also be limited to, typically, a specific gigabyte allowance. You may also be allowed to purchase extra storage, if required, for an additional monthly fee. In answer to the question *"How do I know how much storage I will need?"*, it will be best to ask your vendor. On a desktop or self-hosted system, these storage limitations are only based on your available desktop or server-drive's capacity.

User roles and permissions

In a team environment, user roles and permissions can be very important. They establish how each type of user can interact with each type of record. For example, while a team member may have permission to view and edit contact records, they will not have permission to either delete or export these records. You may want all team members to view and edit records, as this is a part of having team-collaboration capabilities. However, you may not want other team members to be granted access to view your e-mails. Permissions on some SCRM systems can be very robust, allowing multiple permission levels on quite literally every piece of data (records) within the system.

Contact records

While having a contact record would seem to be a fundamental feature of an SCRM (it's not fundamental; it's required), there are many applications that market themselves as SCRMs that do not feature contact records. While these products might have CRM-like functionality and might even bring added capabilities to your SCRM, they are more commonly integrated as third-party applications to SCRMs.

Another important item to consider is the number of contacts that you wish to maintain in your SCRM. It is not unusual, particularly for cloud-based applications, to have limitations on the number of contacts that you can store based on the price level of the product that you choose. In other words, more contacts may equal a higher monthly fee per user. Typically, as people are generally associated with companies (accounts), one company with 10 employees would be considered to be 11 records (10 people + 1 company).

Social CRM can add another element to this equation, and it can be a substantial one. If you follow, for example, 20,000 people on Twitter and you choose to create contact records for each, and if they are not associated with any other contact record, those standalone Twitter followers can count as one record each.

If this does become an issue, you may wish to add folks, such as your social connections, on a case-by-case basis. For that matter, there is a strong argument to be made that everyone in your contact list need not and should not be maintained in your SCRM. People and companies that are either your clients or prospective clients need to be in your SCRM. After that, who you feel the need to create a contact record for is really a matter of personal preference.

Custom fields

Every SCRM will come with a certain number of predefined fields (name, phone, e-mail address, and so on), and their selections are generally fairly robust. However, you will very likely wish to maintain certain information that might be unique to your small business. Assuming this to be correct, you will want to create custom fields for your use only. You will also want to be able to configure different field types (date, currency, drop-down lists, and so on). The number of fields that you will need to create may also be important, and you will want to have the capability to create more fields as your needs arise, so make sure that you will have room for growth.

You may also wish to group your custom fields by that to which they relate. An example might be billing information, shipping instructions, and terms for payment. This might be accomplished by setting up a new tab called *Billing & Shipping* within a contact record. Inside this tab, you would have multiple custom fields that relate to the data needed. On the other hand, your system may allow you to custom design the layout (visual appearance) of your records themselves. In this case, you will be allowed to order and insert fields into a record based on whatever placement makes the most sense for you and for your small business.

E-mail and calendar integration

Many (not all) SCRMs will allow you to generate e-mails as well as create and maintain a calendar of events and tasks. Connecting these to your existing accounts may be a somewhat technical task. Whether or not you might need to solicit professional assistance to accomplish these tasks will vary by SCRM. In other words, some SCRMs are very simple in design and will walk you through this process, whereas others might ask you to enter a variety of variables, which to some (including me) might make little to no sense.

As a basic rule (and this will also differ by SCRM), the common protocol e-mail configuration is either POP3, IMAP, or Exchange. POP3 is an older format that appears to be phasing out. You will need to configure your existing service to allow for the appropriate protocol in order for it to connect to your SCRM. For calendars, typical connections would include those offered by Google, Apple, and MS Outlook.

What happens if you frequently manage your e-mails or your calendar from another platform? For example, I am a Google Apps user and I do the bulk of these entries from my Google interface. Others feel the same way about Outlook or Apple Mail. This answer can vary widely. In the case of e-mail, you may have to copy your external e-mails (those not created from within the SCRM) to a *bcc* address that directs e-mails to your SCRM. The SCRM will then find and attach that e-mail to the correct contact record. A nicer, although less common, feature is some level of *synchronization*.

Synchronization

Synchronization, if available with your SCRM, can be found for e-mail, calendars, contact and account records, and your social networks. There are two types of synchronization, which are as follows:

> ➤ **One-way**: In this case, records or entries created or edited in one system will automatically be duplicated in your other system. For example, contact records created in my SCRM will automatically also be created in my Google contacts but **not** the other way around.

> ➤ **Two-way**: Anything that is done in one system will automatically be duplicated in the other.

Why is this important? Think about how you do business daily and how you want to do business. I e-mail a lot from my phone, and I don't want to have to bcc every e-mail to make sure that it goes to a contact record on my SCRM. The same feeling holds true with my calendar. Two-way synchronization between my SCRM and other platforms and devices takes care of this for me. I also want to have all of my contacts on my phone, but what if my SCRM does not sync these both ways or even one way? In this case, you will want to create your contacts in one system and then regularly export new contacts (or modified contacts) to your SCRM. There may be a third-party application to assist you with this task.

These services can also be either *push* or *pull*. Most smartphone applications these days offer push services. This means that new updates are automatically populated to your phone application. Ding! You've got mail! Pull services will require you to hit a refresh button or schedule a task to do this automatically (say, every 15 minutes) in order to pull in new e-mails or social engagement opportunities, for example. This would be very similar to a traditional desktop application such as Outlook's *new e-mail* routine. *Push* is very nice, but *pull* is still very workable.

Mind you, none of this is really difficult stuff. It's just important that you be aware of your SCRM's potential limitations so that you can develop routines to address those. In a perfect world, you would complete 100 percent of your activities from within your SCRM, and your SCRM may even have those capabilities, but I've never seen a perfect world, and you likely are yet to see one for yourself.

Workflow management

While this is a more advanced feature that may or may not be needed by your small business, workflow management allows you to automate certain tasks that would otherwise need to be done manually. An example would be the dispersion of new leads to assigned salespeople. If you have a multistate sales force, you will assign leads based on the location where this lead originates. You can create a rule that where the lead shows the contact's state or zip code, and that lead is automatically assigned to the salesperson who handles that particular territory.

General company needs – application

Application needs refer primarily to how you want your SCRM to actually look and operate in your small business. This will include desirable features that will provide you with more advanced capabilities.

Dashboard

Think of a dashboard as the home page for your SCRM. Ideally, your dashboard should give you a quick view of what *is* happening now and what *needs to* happen now. Examples might include your scheduled tasks and meetings for the day, as well as your hottest deals and social-engagement opportunities. A manager's dashboard will include team views. Your SCRM might have no dashboard, or it might have one that comes standard with the system or one that you can configure for your own needs.

Tags

Tags are often used to group records together by a common denominator. In some cases, record fields might serve this purpose. For example, if I have a field in an opportunity record that is called "Lead source" and then I choose a source from a list of predefined selections (call-in, tradeshow, cold call), I should have the capability to look at all leads that were generated by an individual source in the form of some sort of a report.

Tags can take these groupings a step further by allowing you to create and assign tags on the fly and quite easily. Multiple tags can usually be assigned to the same record. Depending on how your SCRM is packaged to handle tags, you might click on a tag and call up all records that have been tagged as such, or you may also have the ability to create searches based on that tag in combination with other search parameters.

Search

Most SCRMs are configured to handle basic searches (contact name, account name, and so on). Advanced search is another common feature. With advanced search, you may be able to do things such as the following:

> ➤ Conduct a search based on one or more tag selections as well as other fields. For example, you may have tags created for *industry* and for the *level of interest* that a contact may have to do business with your company.

> ➤ You are also making a trip to Seattle, Washington. Conduct a search for records that are tagged as "Architect" (industry), "Hot" (interest level), and "City" = "Seattle". Now, start calling and scheduling appointments!

The preceding query would be best completed by employing a *Boolean search*, which allows the user to combine keywords using operators such as AND, OR, or even NOT. In the preceding example, we would express this search as follows:

"Find records that contain the tag *Architect* **AND** where the interest level field value is *Hot* **AND** where the city field value is *Seattle*."

Sometimes, advanced searches will allow you to look for a particular word(s) found **anywhere** (in any field) within a specific group of records. This can be particularly useful if you are not sure what field(s) might contain that keyword.

Finally, you will want to be sure that your SCRM's advanced search will also have the capability to conduct searches that will include whatever custom fields you may have created for your own particular small business needs. In other words, it is not unheard of for an SCRM to offer advanced search capabilities based on standard (your SCRM came preconfigured with these) fields only.

Collaboration

Collaboration (allowing team members to work jointly on projects and contacts) is not something that is really all that new, but there has been a renewed interest in this area as a result of social media. While part of this is driven by social conversations, the largest push has come as a result of *social business*. The simple fact is that *social* is becoming more ingrained in all of our business aspects every day. Collaborating with others is a social as well as a business activity. If your SCRM will operate in a team environment, it only makes sense that it should allow for some level of team collaboration. In some cases, as discussed in the previous chapters, this collaboration could be internal as well as external.

Social integration

How your SCRM addresses social integration will be the single most widely differing aspect of any SCRM. There is social and then there is *social*. It's not very difficult, for example, to set up a field with a link to someone's Facebook profile that will take you to Facebook so that you can see that person's profile. That's *social*, right? It must be, because in some SCRMs, that is the entire extent of their social offering. On the other hand, if you want to get *really social*, you will want the following:

> Social profile discovery, where your SCRM will attempt to identify a contact's social networks and then will allow you to connect with them on these networks

> A contact's social profiles to be automatically brought into their contact record

> The ability to see and to engage with what a contact is talking about on their social networks, right now and from within their contact record

➤ Records of our social conversations that automatically become a part of the contact record itself

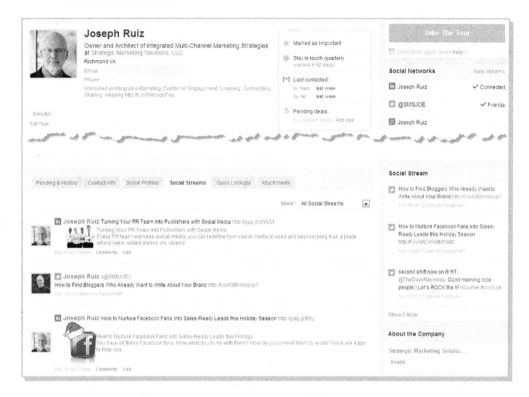

This high level of integration, while not widely found at the time of writing this book, is available. That being said, it is really a matter of what is important to you and to your small business. Some people may find that having access to a contact's social profiles and seeing what they are talking about on their social networks but not being able to engage with them from directly within the SCRM itself will be perfectly adequate for their needs. This may be a decision that you will be required to make for yourself.

Reporting

Not all SCRMs will have reporting capabilities, and even those that do may or may not allow you to print them (if this is even desirable). Those that do offer them might come pre-packaged with frequently used reports. Your SCRM may also provide you with the ability to custom create reports based on your own needs. So, in this case, think about the types of reports that you will require. What data would need to be represented on each report? Then, confirm that your choice of SCRM will allow you to generate these. We would also suggest that you investigate how easy it might be to create your own custom reports, as this is one area where you may or may not require the assistance of the vendor or one of their representatives, and this type of assistance will usually be fee-based.

Third-party integrations

While we will be discussing third-party integrations (applications that talk to each other and share common data) in more detail in a later chapter, if you want your SCRM to be able to integrate with programs such as your accounting system, it will be best to identify that now. Other typical integrations to consider include newsletters, marketing automation, and dedicated customer service/support applications.

Additional frequently found-features

Most SCRMs will include tasks (the ability to create and/or assign a task related to a record), notes (free-type notes into a record), activities (record an activity, such as a phone call, that is related to a record), and events (schedule a meeting related to a record).

In many cases, items such as tasks, activities, and events may be further subdivided as being either held, planned, or not held, which can be handy when you wish to filter these types of activities on either your dashboard or in a report. You may also want or need to group these activities by type. For example, activities might include phone calls, e-mails, or social updates, and you might wish to look at these by group in order to effectively schedule your time.

Sales needs

Recent surveys have reported that over 75 percent of all CRM deployments are focused on the sales force. This is not surprising as CRM has traditionally been a sales-focused application. I would fully expect SCRM to increase this percentage. Salespeople will tend to focus on one issue only: how will the use of a Social CRM make them more money and more effective at what they do best, which should be to sell? A good SCRM will enable them to exceed these goals.

Account type

In addition to basic account and contact information such as name, address, phone, and so on, common fields applicable to sales would include those relating to account type. You will likely wish to identify whether this is an existing customer, a suspect, or a prospect. You might also go as far as marking each account based on their level of importance using the "A, B, C" system, which we first touched upon in *Chapter 1, Exploring the Key Benefits of Social CRM for Your Small Business.*

Other fields or custom fields

These might include industry type or classification, SIC code, date last contacted, referral source, and any other type of information that would be important to *your* small business.

Reminders and recurring reminders

One of the most critical functions of your SCRM will be to remind you of when you need to get back in touch with a client. In the old days, we used "tickler files," which were little more than shoeboxes with 3 x 5 cards and month/day dividers. Now, you will set an electronic reminder to accomplish the same task. Moreover, being able to set recurring reminders is a huge bonus! Going back to our "A, B, C" system, you will want to set recurring reminders to stay in touch with "A" accounts on one schedule (weekly, monthly, and so on) and then do the same for your "B" and "C" accounts on their own schedules.

Managing leads and opportunities is *Sales 101* and a part of that is being able to identify your lead sources. Why spend the time and money on that association membership if it is generating no viable leads? Other important opportunity fields would include the opportunity value; sales stage (where you are in the deal); a percentage chance of closing based on the sales stage; a weighted deal value calculated by applying the percentage chance of closing against the potential value, and finally, whether the deal was a win, a loss, or if it simply went away. You will also want to know the reasons for the final disposition.

Another nice feature to have would be the capability to attach notes, tasks, and scheduled meetings to individual leads or opportunities. Think about it this way; if you are working with a larger company, and particularly, if you have a long-term relationship with this company, you are quite often working multiple deals, and these may also be with multiple people in that firm. Having the ability to create activities and notes that are specific to each individual opportunity, and to keep those separated is a huge plus!

Pipelines and forecasting

Let's just say that it is very difficult to forecast what you are going to sell if you don't even have a firm grasp on what you have working, which sales stage you are in with each deal, what steps you will need to take next, and when you expect to close each opportunity. A good SCRM will effectively manage this. Without all of these, you do not have a forecast. What you do have is a *wish list* and a revenue stream that will closely resemble a small rollercoaster.

Estimates, quotes, and proposals

At the very least, you should be able to attach these documents (and others) to the appropriate records within your SCRM. Some SCRMs will allow you to create quotes and proposals, even pulling and including marketing materials from your online document library and then attaching those to your customer records. As estimating varies so widely by small business, creating and integrating these within the SCRM may be possible but will most likely be found with an enterprise-level solution or via something that has been designed for your specific industry. Still, having the capability to attach a PDF of that estimate to a contact or opportunity record should be available.

Many documents today are being stored online via services such as Google Docs. Your SCRM may offer the ability to attach files via such services.

Social monitoring

This is one major area that will separate an SCRM from a CRM. As a salesperson, I am driven by one thing and one thing only: I want to increase my revenues. We do that by:

> ➤ Discovering new opportunities to solve problems with our products and services for our existing and prospective customers

> ➤ Increasing our connection network base with the right people

> ➤ Generating new referrals from our existing customers

As such, I want an SCRM that will facilitate these goals. What might it mean to you if you were provided with the opportunity to monitor customer conversations in real time, uncover their needs, and then participate in these same conversations while never leaving your SCRM? Might you sell more?

Management

The fundamental goal of every sales manager is to understand where his salespeople and his team are standing at any given moment. This can be done in a variety of fashions, which will be covered in the upcoming sections.

Reviewing individual deal and contact records

Visiting individual records serves two purposes: you can see what is going on, and it may provide you with the opportunity to leave your own comments and suggestions to either handle this account or a specific opportunity.

Dashboards

A salesperson may have an SCRM dashboard that represents a snapshot of what they are working on right now, with tasks and meetings that need to be handled or planned for. The sales manager's dashboard may be very similar, except that it will reflect the activities of the team and its individual members, along with their own personal activities. It is not unusual for dashboards to be separated into tabs (pages), where page one might be your personal information and page two might be reports on your team/team members.

Reports

Reports are used to get a good overall look at team activities and results, and they might or might not include some sort of chart (pie, bar, graph). *Charts only* are sometimes used as the basis for certain dashboards. These reports will be invaluable for planning as well as allowing you to identify trends (good and bad) and then to really zero in on where your salespeople need the most help and development assistance.

In regard to reports, common examples would include activity reports, pipeline reports, pipeline by sales stage, win/loss reports, leads by source, detailed forecasts, and many others. What reports would you like to see? If your SCRM has the ability to create custom reports, the wizards (routines that will walk you through report creation) that are used are generally pretty straight forward, but some outside assistance may be needed. If there is a field within a record, it can usually be inserted somewhere in a report.

Finally, everybody is moving away from paper reports and toward online viewing, so if having a printed report is important to you, you will want to verify that your SCRM has that capability or that you will be able to at least export reports in some usable and printable manner, such as an Excel spreadsheet.

Marketing needs

The most frequent marketing campaigns that are associated with (and are sometimes a built-in function of) CRM will be e-mail driven. This might include a simple *blast* (sending a personalized form letter to one or all segments of your contact list) or a newsletter. Your chosen SCRM may offer other types of campaigns, or it might include none at all. In a future chapter, we will be discussing third-party SCRM integrations and marketing programs. These, including marketing automation, are very common applications.

With SCRM, we now add in the social element, which means that campaigns are extended out to the social channels. Particularly as it relates to SCRM, the ultimate goals of marketing are to create brand awareness, generate leads for sales, and facilitate formal or informal communities of product advocates and ambassadors (fans), which may include influencers (people with established reputations and followers). Once again, as this activity occurs on the social channels themselves, these conversations should be captured and assigned to any previously created contact records.

Campaign creation

Frequent fields associated with campaigns include campaign name, start date, end date, budget, expected and actual costs, expected and actual return in dollars, number of impressions, type, description, campaign goal, a URL that will be associated with tracking this campaign, whether or not to offer an "opt-out" link (this may also be part of a contact record), and a target list to send to. While they're not as common, some systems will also allow you to create and manage SMS (short message service) or text-messaging campaigns.

Social campaigns will leverage the reach that is associated with the social channels and will include links that direct readers to landing pages and calls to action. The goal, in this sense, will be the same as e-mail and newsletter campaigns: create interest, drive people to a site location, and elicit an action that will allow us to capture contact data that will then create either a lead or contact record within our SCRM.

E-mail and marketing templates

Staff might also be involved in the creation of templates that may be used by marketing, sales, or customer service. These templates will allow for personalization of messages and materials as well as being able to pull marketing collateral from our online document library.

Campaign responses

Responses to campaign inquiries may be handled via a variety of methods dependent on the type of campaign and the responsibilities associated with it. For example, marketing materials may be mailed, or they may also be delivered electronically and automatically via a download process. Messages received via the social channels will be responded to in kind and might or might not involve the creation of records within your SCRM, followed by assignment to another department, such as sales, for follow-up.

Communities

Communities might include groups on the social networks or private company user groups. This would also include pages found on the social networks. These services may be incorporated into some smaller SCRMs, most likely Facebook pages.

Management

Marketing management will likely be focused on two things and those are what are the results, and if the results are not what we had anticipated, how fast can we be alerted to this and what can we do to correct or improve?

Campaign results

You will want to have the ability, as it relates to e-mail campaigns, to track messages sent, attempted, and bounced; messages viewed; linked images clicked; click-through links that direct to landing and other pages; opt-outs; leads created; contacts created; and who this lead has been assigned to.

Similar results will be available for social campaigns, although much of this information will be gathered by website analytics such as Google Analytics and/or via link-shortening and tracking services such as bit.ly, Buffer, or Hootsuite (dependent on what you will use to conduct your social campaigns). Data from these services may or may not need to be hand entered into your SCRM. However, third-party marketing automation services (such as Marketo, HubSpot, Infusionsoft), if integrated with your SCRM, can do this for you.

Management will use this information to gauge the effectiveness of campaigns and then to make any needed adjustments, perhaps even mid-campaign, to maximize that campaign's results. Reports that will aggregate these results should be made available.

Customer service needs

Customer service is a natural fit for SCRM; however, not all SCRMs will offer features that are dedicated toward this task. If you are servicing existing customers and this number is manageable, it would be my opinion that related activities become a part of a contact or account record. If you are servicing tens of thousands of transactions, and this is more of a *one and done,* that may not be practical, it does not mean that you do not provide the service. It means that you do not create a customer record for each case.

Is customer support a profit area? If not, it should be! This is a key area in terms of exceeding customer expectations; it is essential that you focus in particular on customers who will buy more from you and/or refer others to you. Not only that, there may also be direct support revenues such as parts, labor, and service agreements.

Cases

If you are going to be utilizing your SCRM for customer service, you will create a different type of record: cases. Typical fields within a case record might include case number description date on which it was created assigned to, priority, case status, type of case, description, notes, time and date last modified, resolution date, and date closed.

There should also be a vehicle to move these to sales whenever an appropriate opportunity is identified. If your company offers warranties and service agreements, data regarding this should also be a part of the record.

Monitoring

People are using the social channels more and more to request service for products and services. Sometimes, this means that they will attempt to reach out to you directly with their request. Other times, they will reach out to you indirectly by telling others how unhappy they are with you and your products. Either way, you will need to respond. Many companies are now creating Twitter accounts that are strictly used for customer service; they are also dedicating sections of their Facebook pages (and others) for the same purpose. Make it easy for your customers! Food for thought.

If your SCRM will be very strong socially, you may have the capability to create your brand-mention searches on the networks. You'll discover these conversations, create records including these conversations, and then create tasks to ensure their follow-up. If not, the monitoring and discovery will need to be managed away from your SCRM and then manually entered into it when each case arises. However, third-party customer service-dedicated applications are very frequent integrations with many SCRMs. If this is of interest or importance to you, you will need to do your research.

Management

The customer support manager will have very similar needs to that of the sales manager. Substitute the word "cases" for "opportunities" or "contacts" and the word "agent" for "salesperson." Now, carry this through to reports and dashboards. The customer support manager will want to keep their eye on both closed and open cases by priority, type, status, and agent.

Should your SCRM be mobile?

The simple answer is yes. Having mobile access to your files, while important to everybody, will be particularly critical to your field sales staff regardless of whether or not they might travel outside of the immediate area. This access might be available via a mobile application from your vendor or from a third-party application from another supplier.

With regard to native applications, these may be offered on one or more of the following platforms. Do not assume that if it is available for one, it will be available for all.

> ➤ iPhone
> ➤ iPad
> ➤ Android phone
> ➤ Android tablet
> ➤ Windows phone
> ➤ BlackBerry
> ➤ Windows tablet

You will want to make sure that your chosen SCRM is available for access from all of your devices as well as what capabilities each will provide. It is not reasonable to expect that everything that you can do from your desktop or laptop, you will also be able to do from a mobile device. Keep in mind that you are dealing with a limited screen size, and therefore, these applications are most often designed to address your most frequent tasks such as looking up contacts, contact notes, creating tasks, and sending and responding to e-mails. However, I have seen some mobile applications that are read only. You mobile application's features might even be tied directly to what package level (Beginner Edition, Standard Edition, Professional Edition) you have selected from your chosen SCRM vendor. We will discuss editions in our next chapter.

Should your chosen vendor not offer a native application for your mobile devices, you may still have the ability to access a web-based version as you would from your desktop. However, every smart phone these days already has contacts, calendars, e-mail capabilities, and even social networking as built-in functions. Therefore, if we have access to these functions, having a native SCRM app may not be as critical as one might think.

Your needs recapped

Now that we have an overview of your needs, it is time to take action by developing a matrix that you can use to document and organize your needs and then to compare how each SCRM that you will consider matches up to those needs. We would suggest a simple Excel spreadsheet. Consider assigning a point system to this matrix, awarding two points where a *needed* feature is present and one point where a *nice* feature is found. *Not needed* or *not available* features receive zero points.

This is important. You might personally feel that certain features are absolutely necessary, while others may provide absolutely no benefit whatsoever. However, you might find that those who will be actually using the system every day have an entirely different view of what is and what is not needed. Therefore, sit down with your team in order to develop and refine this list. Once it has been compiled, sit down with them again in order to create a final comparison sheet.

In our next chapter, we will be discussing other important considerations to choose your SCRM, and vendor columns will be added once your selection process has begun. A sample of this spreadsheet can be found at http://adaptive-business.com/small-social-book-links/.

	A	B	C	D	E	F	G
				ABC Company - Social CRM Vendors			
Feature		Need Level	Vendor A	Vendor B	Vendor C	Vendor D	Vendor E
# Users		5	up to 50	unlimited	up to 10	up to 100	unlimited
# Contacts		3,000	up to 3,000	unlimited	unlimited	up to 10,000	unlimited
Storage Allowance		5 GB expandable	3 GB total	unlimited	unlinited	5 GB per user	10 GB tota;
Contact records / sync		Need / nice	Y / N	Y / N	Y / one-way	Y / N	Y / two-way
Email integration / sync		Need / nice	Y / N	Y / N	Y / one-way	Y / N	Y / one-way
Calendar integration /sync		Need / nice	Y / N	Y / N	Y / one-way	Y / N	Y / one-way

Summary

The goal of this chapter is to make an exhaustive analysis of your needs as they relate to SCRM. This includes making sure that those who will be using the system have had a more than ample opportunity to provide their input. I cannot personally think of many things that would be more wasteful and potentially devastating than to skip around this step (or do it half-heartedly). Why spend time selecting a SCRM and then finally implementing it only to find out later that it just isn't going to work for us? We strongly suggested the following steps:

> ➤ Set realistic goals and expectations

> ➤ Document and prioritize your needs

> ➤ Decide whether or not your SCRM should be mobile-capable

> ➤ Create a simple matrix in order to recap your needs

It is also very important that we learn to think outside of the box and keep a keen eye pointed toward the future. You are probably used to conducting business in a certain manner. SCRM has the potential to challenge these methods dramatically and to provide equally dramatic positive results. Are you prepared for and open to such changes for the better? We hope so! It's kind of like dinosaurs. Either you adapt and evolve, or you die.

This includes planning ahead for your future growth and needs. SCRM, while not overly expensive in terms of a dollar investment, will require a substantial investment of your time to do it correctly. Once again, having to change systems a year or two later as you have already outgrown yours would be... undesirable.

In our next chapter, we will dive deep into the processes of choosing and then implementing your new SCRM. So stay tuned. It's going to be fun and you are getting closer to being able to reap the benefits from your efforts!

Choosing and Implementing Your New Social CRM

We are getting close! In this chapter, we will help you choose a Social CRM for your small business and then will provide you with some helpful and very important tips to ensure a successful implementation.

There are many SCRM choices that are available, and you need to be able to filter through the mass of information in order to determine the right SCRM for you today as well as one that will be able to scale effectively for your anticipated growth and application needs.

In our previous chapter, we asked you to create a spreadsheet matrix of your desired SCRM features. Before we actually get started with choosing your SCRM, we have a few more important areas to discuss, which will have a direct impact on your choice of systems. You will want to add each of these topics to your spreadsheet.

Tip

Be sure to take the time to add these topics to your spreadsheet as they will directly affect your choice of the final system!

Finally, as your other team members have been involved in this project so far, be sure to include them in the process of choosing and implementing your new system.

Choosing your new system

Listed below are the final practical points to consider now that you are ready to begin assessing specific SCRM options.

Desktop versus self-hosted versus cloud-based (software as a service, or SAAS)

There are three common ways to procure and operate your new system. They are as follows:

1. Desktop systems are where the program is typically kept on an individual desktop computer and will be accessible by that person only. This may work for small teams; however, you will most likely not have the benefit of mobile access, team collaboration, or team reporting. These programs are generally purchased for a one-time fee.

2. Self-hosted systems are more like a company network where the software and data will reside on a central company server. While you may own the software based on a one-time fee, it is not unusual for you to purchase, or even rent monthly, seat (user) licenses. In this sense, it is not unlike the SAAS model.

3. SAAS is the new wave of systems where you are basically renting the software, and it is hosted (kept) by the vendor in **the cloud**. Your software is then accessed via an Internet connection. There are many typical advantages to this configuration: low cost, mobile access, software support, and automatic software updates at no charge, although some companies may still charge for periodic updates as either part of an ongoing software-maintenance agreement or on a per-instance basis.

4. There is also a fourth, less commonly found configuration where your software, which you have purchased, will be hosted on a private cloud that you either own or rent. You will get the accessibility advantages of SAAS, and you may also be able to host other programs on the same cloud, thus giving you access to all of your business software via the Internet.

If you are purchasing a system that will not be cloud (browser) based, you will also want to confirm that it will operate on your existing and planned operating system(s). There are vendors that may offer both Windows and Mac-based systems, for example, but it is also not unusual for them to offer their product for only one or the other. Also, confirm with cloud-based systems what their recommended browser(s) will be (Chrome, Firefox, Safari, Internet Explorer). While this is generally not an issue, you may be running certain applications through your preferred browser "X", only to find that the browser may not be recommended to run "Y" SCRM.

There is one other consideration that might affect your system choice; that would be whether or not having your information available to you offline would be of importance. Remember that cloud-based systems are designed to be accessed via your Internet connection. Some cloud systems (not all) will also allow you to download at least basic information to your device so that you can view these records without an Internet connection. Systems that offer this feature will generally even allow you to update records, create and respond to e-mails, add calendar and task entries, and then have these actions completed and synced to the cloud once an Internet connection has been established.

Establishing your budget

For a small business, you can expect to spend anywhere up to a few hundred dollars to purchase software and anywhere from $0.00 per user per month up to say $50.00 per user per month for software subscriptions. Now, you are probably thinking, *"Free??? That sounds good!"* Maybe, but maybe not. As in real life, you do generally get what you pay for. In this case, *free* may mean limited or nonexistent support, a reduced feature set, or maybe even an advertising-supported platform. One thing that we do know for sure is that if a company cannot turn a reasonable profit, it will not be in business for long, which might leave you out in the cold!

Cloud-based SCRMs, particularly for small businesses, will frequently offer what is called a **freemium** model. This is a free version, with limitations, to encourage you to try out the system. As your needs increase (more users, more records needed, advanced features are desired), you will be offered a path to upgrade to a paid subscription version. Don't dismiss this option! Starting out *free with limitations* may still be a viable path for you! Not only does this give you an opportunity to work with the system for an extended period of time, it might even meet your short and long-term needs!

Remember that your investment will be more than your monthly SCRM subscription. There is the time that you will be investing in getting your system going and keeping it running. You may need professional assistance for system installation and training. Hardware costs in terms of a server (if an in-house system) as well as tech support or even just being assured of having good Internet connectivity may also come into play.

Regardless of which system you choose, SCRM for small businesses is typically extremely attractively priced, particularly when weighed against the benefits that you will receive!

Make a note

System packages

It is not unusual to find systems that come in a variety of package configurations, and more features will be included with more expensive packages. Common designations might be Solo, Small Business, Professional, and Enterprise level packages. For example, as a small business, you might even be a solo firm, but there are certain features that you may want and need which will only be available in the Professional level package. So, you may end up investing quite a bit more in order to get those features that you want while, perhaps, also paying for features that you will not use.

Vendor support

SCRM levels of support will vary widely by vendor. Even free systems will generally offer some kind of support system. Support may come in one or more fashions: user groups, support websites with FAQ's and known issues, e-mail support, live chat, or toll and 800 numbers. The bigger question will be centered around responsiveness: how quickly will that vendor respond to any support request? We have seen this range from a few hours to even a week or more. You will want to research this and, if possible, find and talk to users. This can often be accomplished with a simple Internet search that will uncover user forums for the product that you are considering.

Your vendor may also offer paid-support options, which will allow you to use a toll-free number and/or will guarantee a response to tickets created within "x" period of time. Alternatively, as you may be investing in your system by going through an independent approved vendor, they may offer support including helping you with setting up your new system.

There are other support issues to consider. If you purchase the software (versus renting on the cloud), software updates will typically be your responsibility. Your vendor may offer free upgrades, free upgrades for the first year only, or free upgrades with a paid service contract. Ask! With cloud-based software, updates are generally included at no charge. Your local hardware (PCs, servers, tablets, phones, and so on) will always be your responsibility, as will providing a solid (high-speed DSL or cable) Internet connection for cloud-based systems.

Backup and security

If your system will be on-site, you will need to ensure that your data is backed up daily and is securely locked away in some manner. Cloud-based systems face a different set of potential issues not only in terms of backing up data, but also with regard to secure connections and data encryption.

You will likely be relying on your cloud-based service provider to back up your data. Ask them what that means should your data be lost or corrupted in some fashion. What about if you choose to no longer subscribe to their service? Will you be able to take your data with you? What data will be included (contacts, notes, tasks, and so on)? How is this accomplished? How will you know that your data will be deleted from their files once you have left?

 Make a note

An important question for any application that is Internet based is, "What level of encryption is provided? Can the site be accessed via a secure HTTPS connection versus an unsecured HTTP connection?"

Importing your existing data

While we will discuss this in more depth in the next section, the good news is that every SCRM that we have seen will allow you to import your existing records from another source (your existing e-mail provider, current CRM, or even a mailing list), provided that this source will allow you to export those records.

What types of records will you be importing? While this would certainly include contact records (accounts and people), it might also include leads and opportunities, support cases, and campaign records. You will also need to decide whether or not to only import records that are still active. In other words, while you may wish to import records of converted opportunities, will you want to do the same thing for closed support cases or completed campaigns?

Being able to export and then import other data such as history, notes, calendars, and e-mails exchanged is not always an available feature. However, certain third-party applications that are commonly called *data connectors* may be available to assist you with this process, and these are discussed in *Chapter 8, Enhancing Your Social CRM with Third-Party Applications and Integrations*.

You may still choose an SCRM that does not allow for this capability. In that case, you will want to maintain your existing system as a legacy for reference purposes, and/or you will need to manually recreate this data in your new system. Eventually, you may find that the legacy data is no longer of value due to its age.

Ease of use

We cannot stress enough the importance of finding a system that will be easy to use and intuitive by design. In our experience, many systems will fail simply because they are so difficult to navigate that your people will be unable (or unwilling) to use them correctly, if at all. Certainly, good training with any system will be a necessity.

In all fairness, just about every system that you will find today is quite usable. You can teach people how to work with any system, and, through consistent practice, they will become accustomed to its features and flow. However, having a system that is easy to use right out of the box will go a long way toward a fast-track implementation and efficient operation. This being said, an easy-to-use and intuitive system will certainly go a long way toward enthusiastic user adoption!

Have your spreadsheet ready!

The spreadsheet that you have created will be used to match your system requirements against those systems that you are considering. It is designed to ensure that your important business needs are addressed completely, consistently, and in an orderly fashion.

How to begin your search

At the very least, you may have a hundred or more systems to choose from. Where do you start? To begin with, you will want to evaluate options that are labelled as being either a CRM or an SCRM. As an application, SCRM can be referred to by many names, and if you are starting out with a search, you will want to include the following terms: CRM, SCRM, Social CRM, Customer Relationship Manager or Management, and even Contact Manager (the term that was formerly used to describe CRM).

The fact is that CRM is an established moniker, whereas SCRM is a fairly new label and one that is still evolving. Many established brands, Salesforce, for example, are not going to shift their identity from CRM to SCRM even though Salesforce offers SCRM features. Try starting with an advanced Google search: *Software Reviews SCRM OR CRM OR Social CRM*. Other sources for application evaluations and advice include the following:

> ➤ Groups and user groups on LinkedIn, Facebook, and Google+.

> ➤ Forums: These would include user forums for specific applications as well as open forums such as Quora where you can pose questions to a wider audience.

> ➤ Websites: There are many websites that specialize in CRM/SCRM reviews. Try this search: *CRM Idol*. This will take you to two sites, both of which are created by ZDNet.com, which is a well-established and respected review source.

> ➤ There are a number of app review sites, such as GetApp.com and G2 Crowd, as well as user reviews in marketplaces, such as the one that is offered by Google.

> ➤ Vendor support sites: These sites might include user forums but will also generally have FAQ sections and other help-related articles. This is a great place to get your questions answered and will also provide you with a feel for the level of support that you can expect to receive from a vendor. If you pose a question and it is not answered, beware! Also, look at other user questions and follow those threads to see if they were answered in a timely manner. Did the vendor jump in and answer the question, or are all the questions being answered by users (perhaps frustrated users) only?

> ➤ Ask your contemporaries. Do you know other small businesses, perhaps, even some similar to your own, who have already deployed SCRM? Ask them for their help. You might even already be in an association of businesses that has been designed specifically for your industry. Post your questions and your request for advice on the social networks, and put you connections to work for you!

Pulling your "system choice" process together

Refer to your spreadsheet and narrow your choices down to no more than 2-3 options. Where questions have not been answered completely, take the steps needed to get them answered. If you find yourself leaning heavily toward one or two products but they seem to be missing certain features that you have deemed to be critical, you might ask the vendor for suggestions, and those might include third-party integration solutions. We will be devoting our last chapter to this topic; however, be aware that a third-party integration might or might not require an additional investment on your part.

	A	B	C	D	E	F	G
1			ABC Company - Social CRM Vendors				
2							
3	Feature	Need Level	Vendor A	Vendor B	Vendor C	Vendor D	Vendor E
4							
5	Cost	not to exceed $50/mo/user	$15/user/mo	$899.00	$399.00	$35/user/mo	$99/user/mo
6	Support	yes, phone	email	800 number	email	email	800 number
7	Platform	Cloud	Cloud	Desktop	Desktop	Cloud	Cloud
8	Operating System	Mac and PC	PC or Mac	PC only	Mac only	PC or Mac	PC or Mac
9	# Users	5	up to 50	unlimited	up to 10	up to 100	unlimited
10	# Contacts	3,000	up to 3,000	unlimited	unlimited	up to 10,000	unlimited
11	Storage Allowance	5 GB expandable	3 GB total	unlimited	unlinited	5 GB per user	10 GB tota;
12	Contact records / sync	Need / nice	Y / N	Y / Y	Y / one-way	Y / N	Y / two-way
13	Email integration / sync	Need / nice	Y / N	Y / N	Y / one-way	Y / N	Y / one-way
14	Calendar integration /sync	Need / nice	Y / N	Y / N	Y / one-way	Y/ N	Y/ one-way

System trials

Most SCRMs that are available today will offer you a free trial period ranging anywhere from 7 to 30 days, and in most cases, no credit card will be required. We would strongly suggest that you avail yourself of these offers! This does not mean that you will want to try out every system that is available. You might rather do this once you have narrowed your choices down to two or three finalists. Before signing up for any free trial, do make sure that you have set aside ample time to fully and completely test the system within the time allotted.

Most system trials will be fully featured and functional and will allow you to upload your existing real data and run the system as you would with any live installation. In some cases, the trial offering may be for a scaled-back version and/or will have some preloaded sample system data that you can play or experiment with. Once you have completed your trial, and specifically for those systems that you eliminated from your final contention, be sure to cancel your account and verify that they have deleted your data.

Implementing your new SCRM

The next critical aspect of your Social CRM project will be to ensure that it is introduced into your company in an orderly and effective manner. Dropping it in the collective laps of your team and saying *"Here you go. Have at it!"* is a guaranteed recipe for failure. The following is a 10-step program to successfully implement your new small business SCRM. It is also important at this time to have identified your system administrator, who will be instrumental in getting your system off the ground, training your users, and managing your day-to-day system maintenance and upgrades.

1. Determine whether or not you will need professional assistance in one or more of the following phases.

2. Create a system rollout plan.

3. Define your processes (how things work in your small business, or should work, as it pertains to sales, marketing, and customer support) and develop your plans for training.

4. Create the needed custom fields in your SCRM.

5.   Create user accounts and establish permissions.

6.   Connect e-mail, calendar, and social networks.

7.   Decide what reports you will need and what they will include.

8.   Prepare and then import your existing data into your new system.

9.   Test, evaluate, and troubleshoot your data imports.

10. Train your users, starting with your system administrator first.

If and when questions arise during this process, your two best friends will be the vendor's support site and Google or any other search engine. Learn to use both! My personal experience has been that general searches will often take me directly to the associated pages on the vendor's support site and will do so much more quickly than attempting to wade through a support site.

Professional assistance?

Will you be a do-it-yourselfer, or will you want professional help? Much of this might depend on the complexity of your small business and whether or not you have an existing data system (which can be as simple as your e-mail client and contact list) that you will want to move to your new system. Professional assistance may be considered for any or all of the 10 steps of the implementation process.

You can probably expect to pay upwards of $100/hour or more for these types of services. Not cheap, but it would be a reasonable expectation that it will be done right and in an accelerated time frame. You will need to weigh this fees against the value of your own time, that of your team, and your level of confidence in being able to perform these activities correctly and effectively.

If you do enter into an agreement with a consultant, be sure to clearly define your expectations when agreeing to fees. Recognize that your involvement in terms of answering questions and defining needs will be an absolute must. No consultant can read your mind. You must be prepared to direct them.

Create a system rollout plan

As the old saying goes, *"If you fail to plan, you plan to fail"*. You simply have to have a plan, and that plan will include (for each phase) the following:

1.   The order of operation for each phase of your plan.

2.   Assets (personnel and otherwise) that will be required.

3.   A projected start and end date.

4.   Criteria that will determine whether or not this part of your plan has been completed correctly.

When developing a system rollout plan, it is generally considered best to start out with the basics and then build out from there. This is not a race to the finish, and you do want to allow your users to become comfortable with the day-to-day operations of the system before venturing into the more advanced functions.

You might wish to break your plan into phases and have dates for start and completion associated with each phase. Here is an example.

Phase 1 - Completing the steps found in this chapter. As a suggestion, Phase 1 might only include importing and working with account and contact records.

Phase 2 - Import your leads and opportunities and begin to track those through your pipeline. Begin to work with sales reports. Import your support cases and start working with those.

Phase 3 - Import your existing marketing campaigns and work with both support and marketing reporting.

Tip

Every phase must include the needed training and allow the time necessary to practice working with each new feature (or process) that has been introduced.

Define your processes and develop your plans for training

When we think about *processes* in a small business, this may sound like something that is overkill. "*Hey, we are small enough that we don't need bureaucratic rules and procedures. We just do it!*" The facts are generally quite different. If they are not, they should be!

A process is merely documenting what is to occur when a specific trigger action takes place. For example, what happens when a lead is generated? Where does it go and what are the steps that need to be taken in order to turn this lead into a bona fide opportunity? Then what? Actually, *who* and what? Think of each and every step that must be taken and be sure to document how all of these will interact with your SCRM:

➤ Where do leads come from?

➤ Who enters the lead into the system and what information is needed?

➤ How are these moved from the status of a lead to that of an opportunity?

➤ Once an opportunity is created, how do we move it through the pipeline stages?

➤ What information is needed to create and manage your sales forecast?

Make a note

These processes (for all aspects of your business) can first be diagrammed on a piece of paper or even on a whiteboard. After that, document the steps for each and every one. This will become a roadmap for your business, will be instrumental in your initial SCRM user training, and will be your foundation to train new personnel. For many small businesses, just going through this exercise is a very eye-opening experience and one that will be highly beneficial!

Create the needed custom fields in your SCRM

Why is this important to do now? For one reason, if you will be importing data from your existing system and some of that data is fields from your existing system that are not yet present on your new system, that data will have no place to go. You will also need to make sure that your new custom fields are configured to handle the type of data that you want to bring in (dates, text, numbers, and so on) and that the capacity of each field ("x" numbers of letters or characters) will be sufficient for your needs.

Create user accounts and establish permissions

Adding and deleting user accounts should be a fairly straightforward process. You and your system administrator should be the only ones who will be authorized to do this. It will be important for you to have a record of and the control over assigned user passwords.

In terms of setting user permissions, how this is set up will vary widely by your choice of SCRM, and this could range anywhere from "no permission levels and selections" to a very robust offering. Your SCRM should certainly provide how-to reference articles, most likely in their support site, for the proper configuration of this feature.

Connect e-mail, calendar, and social networks

You will want your system to be operational for your users before you begin to train them, and this should include connecting their e-mail accounts, calendars, and social networks. You will likely need their involvement in this process due to the need for user names and passwords that will be associated with their own personal social networks (assuming your SCRM will have this capability).

Connecting e-mail accounts and calendars can range from being something very simple to do all the way to something that may be quite technical. How complex this task will be is going to be dependent on a number of factors, which are as follows:

1. Your choice of SCRM and how it handles e-mails and calendars. Whether or not your SCRM will be cloud based or on-site can have a dramatic effect on this.

2. Your e-mail provider/client (exchange, Gmail, Yahoo, and so on).

3. How you wish your e-mail and calendar to work with your SCRM and other programs or devices.

Things to think about:

> ➤ Where do I want to create and reply to e-mails? Will that be from inside my SCRM, from my regular e-mail client (Outlook, Google, and so on), or both?

> ➤ Is it important to me that e-mail conversations be attached to contact records (I think that it is) and how will we need to facilitate that?

> ➤ Answer questions 1 and 2 again, but this time, for your calendar events and tasks.

> ➤ What about mobile? What will the process(s) be for laptops, smart phones, and tablets?

Your SCRM support site should have extensive documentation for this process. The good news is that if you should find this task to be overwhelming, any decent IT person should be able to configure this for you, and they will be able to do so very easily and quickly.

Decide what reports you will need and what they will include

If your system comes pre-programmed with all of the reports that you will be requiring, at least to start, then you are good to go! If, on the other hand, you will be creating custom reports, then now is the time to begin thinking about those. However, your ability to fully test and polish these reports will be contingent on having the necessary data in your system. As you are just getting started, this data will likely not be present. Therefore, while it is fine to create your report formats at this time, you will likely need to make time available later for testing.

Here is a sample of a deals pipeline report that includes the deal's name, company's name, amount, stage, expected close date, and the weighted value of the pipeline. The weighted value is calculated based on each individual deal amount times the percentage chance of closing. That is, a $10,000 deal with a 40% chance of closing has a weighted value of only $4,000.

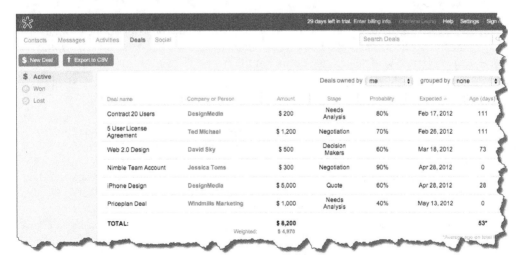

Deal name	Company or Person	Amount	Stage	Probability	Expected	Age (days)
Contract 20 Users	DesignMedia	$ 200	Needs Analysis	80%	Feb 17, 2012	111
5 User License Agreement	Ted Michael	$ 1,200	Negotiation	70%	Feb 26, 2012	111
Web 2.0 Design	David Sky	$ 500	Decision Makers	60%	Mar 18, 2012	73
Nimble Team Account	Jessica Toms	$ 300	Negotiation	90%	Apr 28, 2012	0
iPhone Design	DesignMedia	$ 5,000	Quote	60%	Apr 28, 2012	28
Priceplan Deal	Windmills Marketing	$ 1,000	Needs Analysis	40%	May 13, 2012	0
TOTAL:		**$ 8,200**				53*
	Weighted:	$ 4,970				

Prepare and then import your existing data

You will want to ensure that your existing data is as clean as possible prior to doing any imports. *Garbage in = garbage out*. Specifically, you are looking for duplicate records, typos and misspellings, and data that is not in the correct field (city in state field, and so on).

There are two different ways in which you can clean this up prior to importing to your new SCRM, or you can choose to clean it up later (not recommended):

1. Go record by record in your existing system, and clean each record one at a time.

2. Export your data to a spreadsheet and then clean it up from there.

Your existing system may help you find duplicates (Gmail, for example, will find and merge duplicates); however, it will do nothing about the rest. A data export may also help you identify duplicates (in Excel, *Data | Data Tools | Remove Duplicates*), but merging those may be another matter. Personally, I think that the best and fastest solution is to have your existing system do what it can in this regard and then to use a spreadsheet to edit the rest. Unfortunately, if you have a lot of records, this task is going to be tedious. Regardless, doing so is extremely important!

There are four general ways that a new SCRM will accept imported data from another source; they are as follows:

1. If you are really lucky, your SCRM will have already established a pre-mapped import routine for exported data from your existing system. The most common routines are for Outlook and Google.

2. If your specific system data has not been pre-mapped, your new SCRM may offer what is referred to as a *mapping routine*. In this scenario, your new system will look at each field of data and try to identify and match it with the correct field in its system. For example, you may call this "e-mail" while your new system might call it "e-mail address". For those fields that it cannot match, it will ask you to make that choice for it. These types of routines are generally very efficient and easy to use.

3. You may also have the option of working with a *data connector* application, as we will discuss in *Chapter 8. Enhancing Your Social CRM with Third-Party Applications and Integrations*. Import2 is one such tool.

4. If you are not able to take advantage of any of these options, you will need to perform your import manually.

Performing a manual import is generally not that difficult, but if you have not done one before, it may or may not be something that you might wish to consider farming out to somebody else. There are companies that will offer to perform these tasks as a service. A CRM/SCRM vendor, an I.T. company, or even a printing and mailing company that has extensive experience with working with mailing lists may do so. The level of difficulty will also be determined by how your existing system stores and organizes this data. In order to help you determine whether or not performing this process yourself is something that you wish to tackle, here is the basic process.

Once your data has been cleaned up, you will want to create a file for export. The commonly accepted format to import and export data is in a .csv file format. CSV stands for Comma Separated Value, and this format is a type of Excel file, but it is not the same as a standard .xls file. Once you have exported this file data, make a copy of it and stick your original in a safe place just in case it is needed later.

The first row of all .csv files contains the heading that identifies what the data is in the rows below each column. You will need to match the headings on your exported data file to be **exactly** the same as those headings that are found on your new system's export file template.

What does that mean? If your new system calls the e-mail address "e-mail1", you must rename your appropriate column to be "e-mail1". For some systems, **exactly** also means that the letters are case sensitive. You will never go wrong with exact duplication. Your current or your new system may also require the field values to be combined or separated. For example, your current system may list the first name and last name combined into one field, whereas your new system places the first name in one field and the last name in another. Detailed instructions to split fields as well as convert text to columns can be found at http://bit.ly/1bxczVJ.

In most systems, if your new system cannot recognize any part of the data (it has not been named to match or mapped) being imported, that field will be ignored as will blank fields or columns.

Test, evaluate, and troubleshoot your data imports

Your final step will be to *do a test import* of your existing records prior to performing a complete import. Make sure that these records contain data in every field that will be imported. This is the only way that you will be able to confirm a complete and accurate import. As this is only a test, temporarily adding data to fields, if needed, will be perfectly OK:

1. Make a copy of your edited file.
2. Delete all but the first six rows of your edited file. This will leave you with your headings (row 1) and five contact records.
3. Find the area of your SCRM that facilitates file imports and import your test file.
4. Check each of your five records for import accuracy. If everything looks good, you can delete those records and do a fresh complete import. If not, you will need to troubleshoot the issue(s) and test again before moving forward.

Train your users starting with your system administrator(s) first

In a previous step, we defined our processes for each department and then documented that. This will be one of the foundations for any good training program. Once again, start with the basics. Your SCRM might or might not come with good user documentation, but you must be prepared to document that which you will need if it is going to be necessary. Think of it this way: what you document now can and will be used to train future users.

Now, there is a huge difference between showing somebody how to do something once and then expecting them to perform this same routine(s) consistently. It will be critical for you to evaluate your team members and their progress with the system and to do so daily! They are probably being asked to learn and perform new behaviors, and the only way to master these will be through daily practice. We will talk about training in more detail in our next chapter.

Tip

Evaluate your progress at every phase of your rollout, make any necessary adjustments, and do not move on to subsequent phases until you and your people have completed and mastered the tasks, activities, and system features of your current active phase!

Summary

The focus of this chapter has been as much about planning as it is about action. Developing a good plan, executing it, and then following up will be your keys to a successful SCRM implementation. As all good things take time, take yours during these 10 initial steps:

1. Decide whether or not you will need professional assistance.
2. Create a system rollout plan.
3. Define your processes and plan for your training.
4. Create any needed custom fields for your SCRM.
5. Create user accounts and establish permissions for each.
6. Connect e-mail, calendar, and social networks for each of your users.
7. Decide what reports you will need and what each should include.
8. Prepare and then import your existing data from your current system.
9. Test, evaluate, and troubleshoot these imports. Make corrections as they are necessary.
10. Train your users beginning with your system administrator(s) first.

We do not make any recommendations for specific SCRM systems in this book due to the fact that every small business has unique needs. However, Salesforce. com has excellent free resources that are available for download, including their "Getting Started Implementation Guide" and its accompanying workbook. Go to http://bit.ly/19zxVCh to download copies for your use as needed. While you will find specific references to Salesforce products, the guides are easily adaptable to any SCRM implementation.

The following two chapters will address best practices for your day-to-day activities with your SCRM, and we will be providing you with tips on how to leverage its use to maximize your ability to increase your revenues and develop the kind of customer relationships that will yield long-term recurring benefits.

6

Training and SCRM Best Practices

In our previous chapter, we discussed the steps that were necessary when choosing and implementing your SCRM. Beginning with this chapter, we will now focus on training your team to maximize the effectiveness of your investment. We will be separating our discussion on "best practices" into two chapters. This chapter will focus on the data-creation and management aspect of Social CRM. In our next chapter, we will explore the social capabilities that are brought about by a full SCRM. Having the ability to perform these tasks effectively will greatly increase your chances to maximize your revenues.

How often have you been forced to say this to yourself, (and be honest…)?

> *"I know that we talked about that, but I forgot."*
> *"I forgot that I was supposed to check back with you in January."*

This list could go on and on. The simple fact is that in the chaos of our day-to-day activities, we frequently forget to write things down or note tasks and due dates on our calendars. This is just human nature. While no SCRM will do these things for you, it can help you automate some functions, and it will give you a central and convenient place to document and set your other tasks and reminders.

In this chapter, we will cover the following topics:

> It starts and ends with great training!
> Get focused and get organized!
> Become proactive!
> The 3 Cs of CRM - contacts, calendar, communications
> Every time you are in a record, you should…
> Scheduling reminders
> Organizing and grouping your contacts and activities
> The "A", "B", "C" contact-classification method
> Managing your sales pipeline , support cases, and campaigns
> Internal collaboration
> Monitoring and reporting

It starts and ends with great training!

In order to gain the most value from your new system, you must establish routines for its use. Through repetition, you create a foundation for success upon which we can then continue to build. Haphazard and unstructured usage will render your investment useless. *Of course, all of this starts with proper training!*

The first thing that you will wish to consider is that you have previously designed the processes for your various departments. As your processes have been established as the best methods to achieve maximum results, you will want to train to each process.

Your next step will be to design your training program. There are several key things that you will wish to consider.

Make these decisions before your actual training begins:

> ➤ Who will conduct the training and what materials/preparation will they need?
> ➤ Where will it be conducted?
>> ➤ In-house or at an off-site location?
>> ➤ What about remote locations (if applicable)? Will you bring folks in, travel to their sites, or conduct training via the Web (GoToMeeting, WebEx, and so on)?
> ➤ In what form will the training be conducted? Live on the application, via slides, or both?
> ➤ What collateral information will you need to prepare? This would include user guides (your custom guides and/or those supplied by the vendor) and quick reference cards.
> ➤ How will you conduct the training? Will it be broken up into modules, and if so, what modules, what are their lengths (hours), and what will be the frequency of training (daily, weekly)?
>> ➤ Is everything in place before the training begins?
>> ➤ Have your people cleared their calendars so that they can attend at the appointed date(s) and time(s). Having people miss training sessions will create a logistical and effectiveness nightmare that you will wish to avoid at all costs!
>> ➤ Have you already set up their user accounts and imported their data?

We strongly recommend that your training sessions be limited to 2 to 3 hours at most and you allow at least several days between sessions. A week would be better. Of course, both of these time frames can be adjusted as you see fit. Your goal is to introduce new features and functions in each session and then allow your people ample time to work with and to master each.

Your system trainer will want to work with each individual during that week to make sure that they are properly absorbing the training and utilizing these capabilities. Assignments can and should be given to each team member that will allow them to practice with the system, and these can also be used to measure their understanding of the system as well as their progress. Start out with the most basic activities and then work your way up to the more advanced ones.

A good format for each training session might be:

1. A quick review of the previous session. Answer any questions, and get any feedback.
2. Introduce the new feature(s) for this session.
3. Answer questions and get feedback from this session.

Training and the continuous reinforcement of previously learned skills will be an ongoing process. Do not rush this! You will need to provide constant support and encouragement. If there is a problem, fix it! If there is a question, answer it! Finally, you will need to monitor and measure how your users are doing with the system and will also need to plan for any additional training and reviewing if necessary.

SCRM best practices

In order to receive the maximum benefit from your SCRM, it is critical that you begin to establish fundamental routines, which can then be consistently applied by every individual team member. The old saying that *"practice makes perfect"* is inherently incorrect. "Practice makes permanent" is much more accurate, so practice the right things!

Get focused and get organized!

Much of this centers on the question, *"Do you want to make great quality contacts, or do you want to make quantity contacts?"*. Quality means that you will religiously keep records up to date, set reminders, and review your records prior to making that phone call, e-mail, or personal visit. Customers appreciate it when you have done your homework and you come prepared!

Tip

For those who have a high degree of urgency (think salespeople), preparation time may present an inherent challenge. However, the potential returns (sales) are enormous! You will have the tools, but they are only good to the extent that you actually use them!

Become proactive!

You can choose to respond to crisis situations, or you can choose to avoid them. One of the most essential functions of a good SCRM is its ability to enable you to stay on top of your customers, your prospects, your suspects, your support cases, and your campaigns, without having important related tasks fall through the cracks. When things fall through cracks, your revenues are sure to follow!

The 3 Cs – contacts, calendar, communications

The core functionality of every CRM/SCRM is its ability to manage what we call the "3 Cs":

1. Contacts: Accounts, people, leads, opportunities, support cases, and campaigns.
2. Calendar: Meetings, reminders, and tasks or other activities.
3. Communications: Notes, e-mails, and *social* conversations.

For all of us, these are already day-to-day activities. In many cases, these activities can be overwhelming, difficult to manage, and especially difficult to manage effectively. SCRM changes that!

Creating records

Many SCRMs will have the capacity to quickly add new records. They might even call it something like "quick add". Usually, these routines will ask for the minimum information that would be needed to create a record: name, company name, and e-mail address.

Unfortunately, the reality is that the same records are rarely, if ever, updated with complete information. This will cripple your ability to properly leverage your system information all by itself. One day, you will turn around and find yourself staring at a massive quantity of incomplete records and wondering what to do. You may choose to limp along with what you have, or you may choose to embark on what will be a major "record update" project. Neither option is a great choice, and both might be avoided completely by creating records in the first place.

When I was a young man starting my career in B2B sales, I was expected to make 30 door-to-door cold calls daily. I was required to walk away from each call with the minimum of a business card for the person who was in charge of buying my particular product. When I returned to the office each day, I was expected to staple these business cards to 3 x 5 cards, add any notes, and organize these into my tickler file to ensure their timely follow-up.

Knocking on doors is hard work! Then, there were the appointments, paperwork, and placing and returning phone messages that also needed to be done daily. I was soon telling myself that I could file these business cards tomorrow. Well, that didn't happen. *"I'll double up on this on Wednesday," I thought. "Maybe I can spend some time on them over the weekend. Good grief! I have 150 cards and records to create and no time to do it. I'll do better with the batch for next week. "*Next week would come along, and the size of my pile of cards would grow larger rather than smaller.

You get the picture. You must be in the habit of creating complete and accurate records right there and then if you wish to have any hope of leveraging these to increase your revenues!

Correct spelling and configuration of names and company names is also extremely crucial! If you were to create a contact record for me and you were to spell my name as "Craig Jamieson," you won't find me later when you search for the correct spelling and typical configuration of my name: "Craig M. Jamieson". The same holds true with company names. If you enter mine as "Adaptive Business Company" (incorrect) and then search for "Adaptive Business Services", you will likely encounter the same difficulty.

Now, if I am not somebody who you deal with regularly, you may assume that you just forgot to create a record. Having done so, you have created a duplicate record. One letter, just one letter, that is not the same in one record as it is in another record = duplicate record. Your SCRM may assist you in avoiding duplicate records by pulling up and suggesting existing records that it already has on file. This is normally done through letter matching where as you start to enter a name, it will pull up records that are already on file based on the letters that you have entered.

Manually removing or merging duplicates can be an extremely tedious task! Hopefully, your system will have some sort of a utility to find and merge or delete these, but regardless, they are the bane of any SCRM. So, take your time and get it right from the start! Not enough time to do that? It's funny how we will always manage to find the time needed to correct something that was not done right in the first place.

Managing your calendar

For many people, their calendars are like *command central*. Mine is certainly that for me. It is how we stay on top of appointments that we have scheduled and reminders that we have set. However, one of the challenges that you may encounter with your SCRM is that it will want to place literally everything on your calendar, including appointments, reminders, and tasks. There is nothing wrong with this in theory. In practice, your calendar will rapidly become so overwhelmed with entries that they will soon be sitting one on top of the other.

Ideally, your SCRM will have two features to assist you with this quandary, assuming that you are faced with it. First, your SCRM should be able to remind you of tasks either via a pop-up and/or an e-mail alert. These items might also appear on your dashboard under the heading of something such as "Daily Tasks". Secondly, you should have the capability to select what appears on your calendar. You may wish to hide tasks and reminders if this feature is available.

Not only do I want to manage my calendar, I'd also like to be able to see what is on the calendars of my other team members—and that might include members who are outside of my particular department. This function is particularly crucial from a collaborative standpoint. Many SCRMs will allow you to invite other team members to events or appointments, and this is much more effective when we can see what their current schedule looks like. You may even want to block out times during the week and mark those as "Available" in order to make it easier for your team to schedule appointments when they know that you will be free.

Recording your activities

Your SCRM will likely allow you to record notes including those from meetings that you may have had with a client or a prospect. The same feature will ideally extend to your team members. There will also be a separate section that is devoted to specific activities such as documenting a phone call that was made or an e-mail or a letter that was sent.

The capability to add notes and activities may extend to other types of records as well. Looking at how records are associated (attached to each other in some manner); you may have a single company record, multiple contact records that work for that company, multiple lead records that are attached to that company as well as its individual contacts, and the same for opportunity records, support cases, and marketing campaigns.

Here is a simple example. I work with the ABC Company, and at ABC, I also conduct business with five different department heads. I might have several deals in a variety of stages with one or more of these people in progress at any given time. Does it make more sense for me to:

> Enter notes on any activity that has occurred just in the main company record?

> Document these activities in the associated person contact record?

> Add these notes and activities to each specific opportunity?

The answer is 3: add notes and activities to whichever record that they are specifically associated with. This is the only way in which you will be able to keep this information properly organized and of any use.

Tip

As with your calendar, be sure to close any activity (if it is an open or scheduled activity) by marking it as having been completed, or if necessary, change the activity due date if you need to move that date out.

Task management and assignment

Your SCRM will likely provide you with the means to set and to view all tasks that you have created. This would include tasks by type and description, open tasks, and completed tasks. Tasks need to be associated with specific records (account, person, lead, opportunity, support case, or campaign).

You also ought to be able to assign tasks and due dates to other team members as well as to review and comment on their open tasks.

Attaching documents

Whenever possible, always attach the electronic version of any document that is associated with a specific record. For example, I would attach an electronic copy of a proposal that was created for a specific opportunity to that opportunity's record. What if your SCRM does not have the ability to attach documents? You have a couple of options:

➤ Create a folder for each customer on your desktop along with subfolders for each opportunity and so on

➤ Store your documents in the same folder hierarchy but on a cloud-based storage system

Make a note

Examples of cloud-based storage systems are Dropbox, Box, Google Drive, iCloud, and OneDrive. These systems all come with an amount of free storage (generally 1 GB or more) and with the option to buy additional storage for very reasonable fees. The best part of this method is that you can typically access each document via a unique link that the storage system will generate for each document. Therefore, create a note that states, "Proposal document can be found at [document URL]".

Every time you are in a record, you should...

Once again, it is critical that the information contained in a contact record be accurate! Therefore, *whenever* you are in a record, be sure to check for the following:

➤ Misspellings

➤ Missing, inaccurate, or out-of-date information

➤ Potential duplicate records

Make a note

If you correct your records as you go along in your day-to-day activities, you will manage to keep a clean database and avoid the massive task of having to spend days righting a database that is no longer fully useable with any degree of confidence.

Now, it's probably a fair guess that you are in a record for some purpose. Take this opportunity to add any relevant notes and tasks, review your previous correspondence as well as these notes and tasks, and always set a reminder for your next contact! If you are getting ready to make a call on this contact, be sure to review all of the above before you walk out the door or pick up that phone!

Scheduling reminders

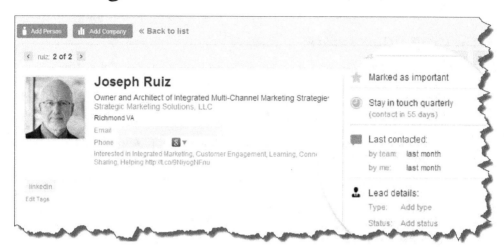

One of the most powerful functions of any SCRM is the capability to set reminders for you to get back in touch with a customer or a prospect. Depending on your SCRM, this may be accomplished in one or more ways:

1. Schedule a reminder to perform a task on a specific date and time.

2. Ask for a reminder in "x" number of days.

3. Set a recurring reminder asking you to be notified on a set schedule such as daily, monthly, or quarterly.

If your system is really smart and you have set a recurring reminder, it will adjust this reminder automatically if you make a customer contact before the scheduled date/time.

Another variation of this function is setting reminders that are based strictly on the date on which a customer was last contacted. We might even want to look at this by the *day last contacted by you* or the *day last contacted by a member of your team*. This could also be part of a structured search as in, *"Show me all contacts who have not been contacted within the last 30 days."*

Organizing and grouping your contacts and activities

There are a number of ways that your small business SCRM may be able to group your contacts. One way to do this is through the use of "type" fields. These are usually fields that will provide you with a preset group of optional selections as a drop-down list, which will ensure that you create these fields consistently. For example, you might have *industry type*, *lead or referral source*, and *salesperson or support person*. This will make it simple to view different groups of contacts together.

Another method is to use tags. You can create these as needed, but your SCRM will prompt you from its record of tags you've used earlier. Tags can also be created for activities. For example, I might create activity tags for *phone call, e-mail,* and *personal visit.* Why do this? Effective time and territory management would be one very good reason. As an example, if I have set time aside to make phone calls, I will be able to call up those based on selecting that tag. If I am heading downtown, I will be able to schedule personal visits that are in that area.

Both tags and fields ought to be searchable, and you should be able to simultaneously search for any combination of tags and fields. This is a wonderful way for you to organize and manage your time. You may also be able to export these searches as either a PDF or a .xls spreadsheet for use in other applications such as e-mail marketing. Let's say you have just introduced a service that would be perfect for manufacturing companies. Create a search for contacts who have been tagged as both *suspects* and whose industry type (field) is *manufacturing,* and start reaching out to share the news!

Would you like to know all of the phone calls that you need to make this week? Search for activity tag, *phone call,* and then search for a *due date* between today and Friday.

The "A", "B", "C" contact-classification method

We touched on this topic in an earlier chapter, but its importance merits additional discussion. Studies have shown that it may take an average of seven calls to a potential customer before you will have an opportunity to even make a presentation. This is particularly true if your prospect is already happily (it would seem) utilizing the services of one of your competitors.

Then, there is the ubiquitous 80/20 rule which, in this case, states that 80 percent of your revenues will come from 20 percent of your customers. We also have to look at why any customer will choose to leave you. They will leave you because, in one way or another, they have felt ignored and/or unappreciated. Given the expense of finding new customers to replace these, this is to be avoided at all costs!

We will begin by separating your active accounts into one of the following four classifications:

➤ "A" Accounts: This refers to companies and contacts who have consistently and repeatedly, generated high streams of revenue. This may include your best customers, but it could also include your top referrers.

➤ "B" Accounts: These would be your second-tier accounts. They do not presently buy as much as your "A" accounts and/or are not presently referring you to others as often as your "A" accounts do.

➤ "C" Accounts: "C" accounts may either be accounts that produce smaller amounts of revenue (albeit consistently), or they may be target accounts that you feel will have the potential to move up the ladder, once a relationship with your company has been solidified.

> ➤ "D" Accounts: "D" stands for "delete". They don't do business with you, and the likelihood of them ever doing business with you is negligible. Get rid of them and find someone better!

You can use tags to identify and group these accounts, or you may use a field record within your SCRM to accomplish the same thing. The next step is to establish a call-back schedule for each of these classifications. While you will need to determine these schedules based on your own experience and needs, one example might be:

> ➤ "A" Accounts – weekly
>
> ➤ "B" Accounts – monthly
>
> ➤ "C" Accounts – quarterly

Assuming that your SCRM allows you to set recurring reminders, set these for each account classification. You may even be able to call up each of these by group and mass update each record with the appropriate call-back schedule without having to do it record by record. If your system does not have recurring reminders, these tasks will have to be done manually. Go to that contact record, update the current reminder as having been completed (providing it has been completed), and then set your next reminder.

Now, going back to the 80/20 rule, how many of your contacts are really "A" Account material? You are going to have to be brutally and realistically honest about this assessment, and you will also want to balance this with your capacity to handle the associated workload. Can you be in contact with 250 accounts weekly? Maybe if you have superpowers. More likely, you will want to limit your "A" Accounts to 25 to 50 at most.

We can work these numbers backward to arrive at a total *active* account number that we can effectively service properly. Let's start with 50 "A" Accounts. In this case, those 50 accounts are equal to 20 percent of your total *active* accounts. This means that you can actively support 250 active accounts only. Maybe 30 percent of your accounts would be "B" Accounts = 75, and the remaining 125 accounts would be "C" accounts.

Finally, you will want to evaluate all of these accounts continuously based on a comparison of their actual status to your established revenue benchmarks. Account status can go up (a good goal with every "B" or "C" account), or it also might go down. If it goes down, why does it? Are they being serviced correctly? Were there changes in management? Whatever the reason, account statuses going down are a cause for alarm and must be evaluated and addressed immediately.

In the long haul, this is all part of what I call "culling and improving the herd." Weak accounts are either eliminated or are handed off to an internal support representative who might be better able to service their needs. This creates room for you to bring in and properly service new high-potential accounts.

Managing your sales pipeline, support cases, and campaigns

As all of the preceding concepts pertain directly to your revenues, being able to manage and anticipate your sales, your support staff needs, and your scheduled campaigns' results is an essential function for any small business! This capability extends out to proper planning as well as to improving your process in any department that might be affected!

Pipelines, funnels, and forecasts

There is quite a bit of discussion about the differences between a sales pipeline and a sales funnel. Don't get caught up in semantics. The bottom line is that we need to move any deal through its various stages with the end result (optimally) being a sale. Here is an example of a simple sales funnel:

We can look at this example in two different ways. One way is that a lot of leads go in the widest part of the funnel (the top), and as those go through the various sales stages, fewer and fewer survive. In other words, some deals go away or are registered as losses.

On the other hand, your funnel is a living and breathing ecosystem. As deals move down the funnel, new opportunities need to be added into the top. We do know three things:

1. If there is nothing in your funnel (opportunities), nothing is going to be coming out the bottom (sales).
2. Opportunities stuck in your funnel are not moving for some reason. What is it?
3. Not every opportunity will become a sale.

The problem with most sales forecasts is that they are based on a salesperson's gut feelings rather than on any objective basis. In this sense, they are more of a "wish list" than anything else. Why don't we change that up by moving away from a *guess* and toward something that we can more accurately quantify? What would it mean to your business to be able to have a revenue forecast that you can count on? How will this affect your cash flow, your inventory-related decisions, and maybe even your payroll?

We can do this by instead evaluating each opportunity based on selling benchmarks having been achieved. Each benchmark equates to a stage in the sales process. Furthermore, we assign a *percentage chance of closing* to each stage. This percentage is applied against the anticipated opportunity value to arrive at a weighted value. For the purposes of a sales forecast, the *weighted value* is what is considered. For example, $50,000 in opportunities, each with a 10 percent chance of closing, is more realistically $5,000 in sales. Here is an example that you can adjust for your own needs and to fit your specific sales process:

10 percent	*A fresh qualified lead or too soon to tell or unlikely to close.*
20 percent	*Client agrees to initial meeting.*
30 percent	*Client agrees to a second meeting.*
40 percent	*Client wants to see your recommendations (proposal).*
50 percent	*Client is qualified and will buy from someone. They have the money, the authority, and the need (M.A.N.)*
60 percent	*Client likes and accepts your ideas.*
70 percent	*Client has declared a competitive preference for us and wants final recommendations.*
80 percent	*Verbal acceptance of the order. While details may be being worked out, they will not affect the final decision.*
90 percent	*You have received a verbal order and are simply awaiting written confirmation and/or the purchase order.*
100 percent	*Order has been received and credit has been approved! Mark this as sold!*

I have used the same basic system for years, and I can tell you, if you are honest in your stage appraisal and follow the process outlined, this does work! You must be sure to evaluate your opportunity sales stage and adjust that within your SCRM regularly in order to get an accurate picture. Remember, it is possible for stages to go down (with a lower percentage chance of closing) and then go back up again.

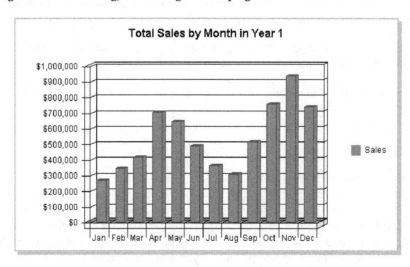

Now, and this is keeping things simple, assign an anticipated close date to each opportunity, group those by month, and then generate a report that reflects sales stage, percentage chance of closing, total and weighted values, and so on. You now have a basic sales forecast that can be formatted as a list, a chart, or both, as is shown in the preceding image. These can also be further divided by team and team member.

This is great information to have, but the devil is often in the details and you will want to look closer. Ideally, on the surface, you have a sales forecast that is telling you that you can anticipate "X" dollars in revenue for any given month that is shown on the report. However, drilling down, how is it that I have a $10,000 opportunity that is scheduled to close this month but that only has a 10 percent chance of actually closing? This would lead me to believe that something is not quite right.

There might be a number of questions to ask. Is 10 percent a correct figure, or has this deal actually progressed further in the sales stage process? Is the anticipated close date accurate or has it never been updated? Does this salesperson even know how this system works or what stage in the selling process they are actually in? Do they even understand how to move this deal along? Yes, a sales forecast can identify many other areas in need of your attention in addition to your revenues! It can pinpoint training needs as well as help you evaluate your sales staff.

Support cases

Managing support cases is really not that different from managing leads and opportunities. In fact, these support cases are often opportunities in disguise. Certainly, your small business's efforts to solve these issues in a correct and timely manner will have a powerful effect on whether or not this customer will continue to do business with you and/or refer your company to others.

Records need to be created. The data for those may arrive via e-mail or from your dedicated support site. From there, as with all records, it will be critical that all of the information contained within be accurate and up to date. Many companies will want to track a variety of data that pertain to these cases including:

> ➤ Time and date received
> ➤ Where the request originated
> ➤ The nature of the issue (which may be subdivided into standard case types)
> ➤ Who has been assigned to the case
> ➤ Case urgency status
> ➤ A trail of what steps have been taken to correct the issue
> ➤ The eventual solution and case completion date
> ➤ Customer feedback regarding the resolution of the case

Finally, I am a strong believer in having each case associated with a contact (account and person) record so that the servicing agent (and other departments including sales, marketing, and product development) will have a record of cases that involve this particular account. Maintaining and interpreting the data gathered in this module within your SCRM properly could very well be the difference between a profitable small business and one that will soon be closing its doors. It's that important!

Campaigns

Important questions will be answered through the consistent and effective use of a campaign module within your SCRM:

> ➤ Which campaigns are working and which are not?
> ➤ How are leads being delivered to sales, and are they being followed up on?
> ➤ Are the sales team reporting results back to marketing?

As it is commonly considered the responsibility of marketing to create and deliver qualified leads to the sales department, you may also want to set up a lead-scoring system and compare these scores with actual results. A simple lead-scoring system involves objectively assigning points to a lead based on a number of factors and events. Given that many opportunities arrive via contact forms that have been completed on your website, these might include the following:

> ➤ The company name
> ➤ The company industry
> ➤ Their number of employees
> ➤ Their annual revenues
> ➤ The title of the individual who filled out the form
> ➤ The number of visits to your site including when, how frequently, and pages viewed
> ➤ Collateral (e-books, whitepapers, and so on) that this individual/company has downloaded

A simple system to document this information might entail creating custom fields on your SCRM. Based on this information and the assigned points, the higher the score, the more qualified the lead would be. Here would be a simple example:

1. Create fields (if you do not already have them) on your contact records for each of the seven areas depicted in the preceding list that reflect the information gathered on your web contact form.

2. Next, create fields that will contain a lead score for each of the fields. For example, you will have a field named "Annual Revenues," and next to it you will have a field called "Revenue Score."

3. Now, you will want to create a point table that will correspond to each of these areas. Using our same "Annual Revenue" example, it might look like this:

Annual Revenues	Points
0-100,000	1
101,000 - 250,000	2
251,000 - 500,000	3
501,000+	4

4. Repeat this process by creating point tables for each lead-scoring area.

5. Finally, total up the points that are found in each field to come up with a total score and create a similar table that will reflect what total you feel would reflect a good lead, an average lead, or a very poor lead.

You may also want to consider criteria such as if they score one point or less in any score category, it may be an automatic lead disqualifier regardless of what their total score might be. You will next want to compare your actual results against your scoring system and adjust your system from there.

Conversely, if people are not visiting your landing pages or they are not completing the contact forms, you will want to know that and understand why this is happening.

Internal collaboration

While your small business might or might not have departments, the last thing that you want to have is silos (departments acting independently while ignoring opportunities to cross-share valuable information). Keep your eye on the goal of exceeding customer expectations!

Your privacy settings and role assignments will ideally allow all team members to view and comment on the following:

➤ Records - contacts, leads, opportunities, support cases, and campaigns

➤ Tasks, notes, activities, and events

Why is this critical? Would it not be nice, before your account representative went out on that call with an important customer, that they be informed about the following:

➤ There is an open order and the status of that order

➤ A pending support case is still being resolved

➤ They need to stop by and visit Nancy while they are there

➤ Their customer recently downloaded a copy of a white paper that had been offered, and this document pertains to some of your services that this customer currently does not utilize

The answer would be yes!

Monitoring and reporting

One of the really great things about any SCRM is having team and individual statistics and information at your fingertips! As someone who spent the majority of his career in management, being able to review my salespeople's activities at any given time is invaluable. I would suggest daily reports, as it is much easier and more effective to plug a leak than it is to rebuild a dike. This information may be available to you via your dashboard, reports, or maybe, even through system-generated alerts. You will be able to do the following:

➤ Gauge team member activity

➤ View upcoming meetings

➤ Assess the status of any deal that is in progress

➤ Determine the status of support cases by team member

➤ Evaluate the effectiveness of active and completed campaigns

The list goes on!

What will you choose to do with this information? While much of this data represents current statuses, it can also be used to assess and address areas where your assistance as a manager or as an owner may be needed. Why is there too little activity? How is it that deals seem to be stuck at a certain stage and have not moved through the sales funnel? Why are so many support cases being filed for this one particular issue? Why isn't Bob following up with leads that have been generated by marketing? Why are the leads being generated by marketing not closing? As we are spending all of this money on lead-generating activities (shows, campaigns, associations, memberships, advertising, Web, social media), where (and where not) are we getting acceptable returns?

Just as you will be able to identify those areas in need of attention, the system will also let you know what is working, and when something is working, we want to replicate it and maybe even improve on those successes!

Summary

In this chapter, we explored many of the best practices that are associated with the CRM aspect of SCRM. CRM, in itself, is a database, and if you are not willing to make the commitment to keep the data clean and up to date, you will have nothing more than an electronic rolodex and one with marginal accuracy at best.

However, if you are willing to pursue the use of your SCRM religiously and make it a reflex part of your daily routine (reflex comes with repetition), it has the potential to return enormous benefits to you and to your small business!

Just think of this: a well-maintained CRM will allow you to have the following at your and your team's fingertips:

> ➤ All client information
>
> ➤ A history of your notes and shared communications
>
> ➤ Open and completed tasks and events
>
> ➤ Opportunities that are in progress

All of this regardless of whether you are at your desk or on the road. This is tremendously empowering! In order to take advantage of this, and this is sometimes a challenge for people who have a high sense of urgency, you will need to learn to slow down and focus on making quality contacts rather than rush just to make that next contact.

Just as important is having the capability to focus on one particular record at a time. This will be even more crucial as we explore the social side of SCRM in our next chapter. One of your ultimate goals is to uncover and then nurture business relationships with others. The real-time aspect of social media will provide you with many ways to do this, and your SCRM will be there to assist you in managing these relationships!

In our next chapter, we will be really digging in to how you can leverage the power of the *social elements* of your SCRM! We will be discussing goals and best practices that you can deploy to build those relationships and to increase your revenues!

Exploring the Social
Elements of SCRM

SCRM puts the "R" (Relationship) back into CRM and becomes the key to building relationships and uncovering opportunities based on your willingness to engage with others. This is the social element of SCRM, and it will result in increased revenues. In this chapter, we will discuss the following topics:

➤ An overview of social best practices

➤ Social sales best practices

➤ Social customer support best practices

➤ Social marketing best practices

An overview of social best practices

As we begin our discussion of SCRM, there are three critical points that must first be addressed. They are as follows:

1. While CRM is a mature application, SCRM is still being defined. In other words, while most CRMs will perform similar functions, SCRM feature offerings will vary widely. Some legacy (established) CRM systems are adding SCRM features to their core long-established platforms, but there is also a new breed of vendors who are building SCRM products from the ground up.

2. The social capabilities and features will vary widely by SCRM vendor, and it is therefore impossible for us to make blanket statements regarding the features and capabilities of any SCRM. You must do your research based on these features, which are important to your small business!

3. There is a strong likelihood that a substantial portion of your social engagement will occur outside of your SCRM itself, and then these contacts and conversations will be added to your SCRM records if and when you deem it to be appropriate. Even with a SCRM that is highly social, the same rule will hold true.

There may be a variety of reasons when working directly within the social networks themselves will be a necessity. By this, we mean there will be times when it will be more efficient, perhaps, even required for specific functions, for you to go directly to Twitter, LinkedIn, or Facebook. A good example for this would be editing your profile on that network or adjusting your privacy settings. No third-party application, including SCRM, will attempt or even see the need to duplicate all of the available functions that can be found in each network.

Your Social CRM goals

Regardless of whether you will engage socially from within your SCRM or from the social networks themselves, your goals (in order) are to:

1. Listen

2. Engage to discover opportunities

3. Establish a more formal connection

4. Move these contacts and engagements to your SCRM by creating the appropriate record(s)

5. Manage them going forward from your SCRM

We cannot overstate the importance of this process! Hopefully, depending on your SCRM, these conversations might automatically be captured to specific contact records. If not, you will need to do this manually.

Maybe this is a good time to more fully explore what constitutes an **opportunity**, of which many will be found by monitoring your social networks. The definition of an opportunity may vary by department, but only very slightly.

If I am in sales, an opportunity might be someone with an identified need for my services, dissatisfaction with a competitor's offering, or an expressed pain point that I can solve with my product or service. Another great opportunity would be connecting with someone who can refer me to others or who might provide me with other valued forms of expertise.

Your customer support department is looking for people who need help with your products or services. Believe me, this is an opportunity! It can create a satisfied customer who will not only buy more, but who will also be a brand ambassador (vocal supporter) of your company and who will refer you to others. As I believe in the axiom that *everybody sells*, customer support is also on the lookout for those same opportunities that are being sought after by sales.

If the goal of marketing is to create brand awareness, generate buzz, and to deliver qualified leads to sales, then there is no better platform to achieve this than on social media. Unlike print and other campaigns, people will talk back to you (or sometimes at you and in a less than complimentary tone). This is *conversation*. These same conversations will spur other people into talking about your product or service (ambassadors and influencers), and these discussions all lead back to *opportunities*.

Tip

Think before you import your social network connections!

 There is probably not much to be gained by importing thousands of people who you follow/are connected to on social networks, *unless* you see an opening to engage and create a relationship that leads to an opportunity. A better process would be to add them to your SCRM as records if and when your contact benchmarks (how you will grade the overall importance of a contact) are achieved.

Enhanced record creation

SCRM will allow you to create and populate additional social network fields to the appropriate records. The most common type of record will be for a specific person. Your SCRM may allow you to add profile URLs to the specific fields that have been assigned to each network. It may also allow you to automatically search and assign social network profiles based on algorithms that will use (among other things) this person's e-mail address and their name.

Having this capability to auto-find social network profiles is a huge advantage. If none are readily apparent with a high degree of certainty, your SCRM may suggest possible matches. At the very least, it will most certainly allow you to manually enter this information. Importing from the social networks themselves might also facilitate this process; however, remember that any import from any network will only be for the people whom you are already connected with.

Once you have found these profiles, your SCRM should also correctly identify whether you are connected to that person and on what level. If you are not connected, it should provide you with the ability to send a connection request (or a friend request on Facebook or follow on Twitter).

If you do not connect each contact's social profiles, you will be defeating the entire purpose of SCRM, so be prepared to invest whatever time is needed to accomplish this goal! Once you have connected social profiles, your SCRM will become dynamic and will provide you with an updated news stream of what your prospects are talking about right now!

Tip

E-mail addresses are (at least at this time) the *glue* that holds social networks together. These addresses are the universal matching mechanism between that individual and their network(s). However, be aware that some people may use one e-mail address for business and a personal e-mail address for social networking, so having both will maximize your chances for a successful profile search and discovery.

Your records become a dynamic resource

As discussed earlier, a CRM is little more than a static database where you can add, edit, or delete information. By connecting social networks to your contact records, SCRM becomes a living, breathing organism. Within your contact's record, you will be able to monitor and engage with them on the social networks in *real time*. What does this mean?

Just the other day, a local person whom I know casually called me up asking me for some information regarding the SCRM that I represent. While we were on the phone talking, I pulled up her record. Her latest tweet asked if anyone had any experience with Google Voice. I came right out and said it, *"I understand that you are interested in Google Voice. Are there any questions that I can answer for you and oh, by the way, our SCRM has Google Voice integration."* As you might imagine, she was both shocked and impressed!

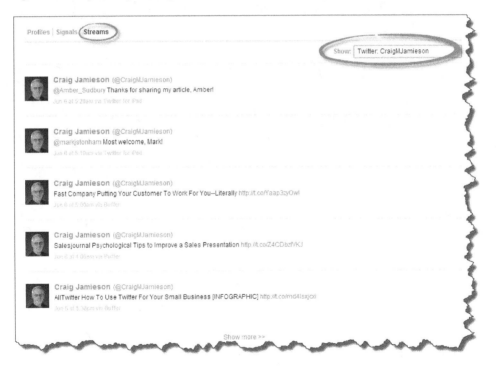

From your contact's social stream, you will hopefully be provided with the functionality to engage where appropriate via replies, retweets, comments, and so on.

Get to know – really know – your contacts!

Being able to engage socially with your contacts is the best way to really get to know them. It's like a neighborhood BBQ without the buzzing insects. You will be amazed at how much you can learn. Once again, who do people buy from? They buy from people whom they know, like, trust, and respect. They also buy from people whom they perceive to be much like themselves or who share common likes and interests. This might be hobbies, it might be that you went to the same university, or that you are friends in common or have a shared love for a particular rock band. It could be anything, and make no mistake, social networking is where folks talk about these types of things all of the time and do so quite openly.

Social activities aggregate to your SCRM

Remember that once you have created the appropriate records in your SCRM and have included your contact's social network profile URLs, any conversation that you have will be aggregated to the appropriate record. Regardless of whether it has taken place on a desktop, tablet, mobile, phone, or third-party application, a good SCRM will record it all. The following screenshot includes e-mails, Twitter interactions, and a Facebook direct message. This is what we would call a *unified message* record.

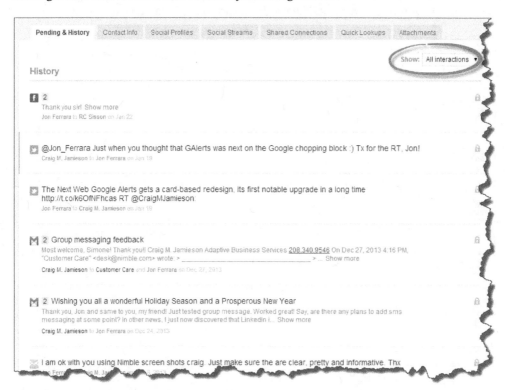

Using your SCRM as your social dashboard

Your SCRM may include some sort of a social dashboard similar to those offered by Hootsuite and Sprout Social. A social dashboard allows you to update to, monitor, and engage with multiple social networks and their activity streams from one central page. A typical example would include the news streams from Twitter, Facebook, and LinkedIn. You may have the capability to even narrow your results down based on groupings such as Twitter lists.

Social dashboards will also offer you the ability to search by keywords and then to save those searches. A social dashboard on an SCRM should expand these capabilities by allowing you to create records and tasks that relate to specific updates that you will either find in the normal course of monitoring the networks or discover via searches.

Perhaps, most importantly, a good social dashboard will notify you of others' attempts to engage with you! What are you going to do then? You might reply in the appropriate manner, you might choose to follow or connect with this person if you have not already done so, you could create a task for follow-up later if this person is requesting help or information, and you might even create a record for them in your SCRM. I can do all of these without ever leaving this page!

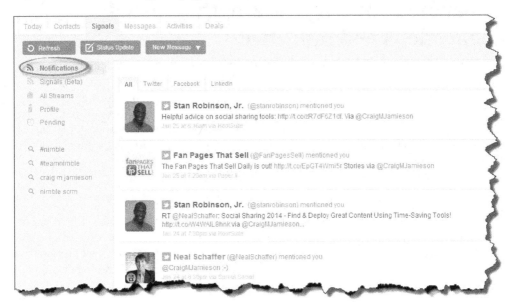

Don't neglect the importance of providing value

Social networking is as much about being found as it is about finding connections and opportunities. We attract others to our profiles and our sites by providing value. In general, value is something that will resonate with your audience and will provide them with a benefit that will then be associated with you.

As a result of this, the leveraging of social media is often called *attraction versus interruption* marketing. *"Like my page on Facebook"* is not value. *"Download our free report of 10 awesome tips to master social selling"* is.

Social selling best practices

Social selling and Social CRM were made for each other. Together, they form a marriage of leveraged traditional and social activities and account management that will undoubtedly increase your small business's revenues as well as your salespeople's commissions! It requires an approach that should be directly integrated into your sales process.

Expanding your network with targeted connections and influencers

Perhaps, we should begin this discussion by defining *targeted connections*. Simply put, it is important for you to connect to people who, in one way or another, can provide you with a mutually beneficial relationship. Examples might include your customers, your prospective customers, people who might refer you to others, folks who are thought leaders in your industry, and maybe even other people from other companies who also work with the decision makers who you might target. In other words, if I want to sell $1,000,000 mainframe computer systems, I'd like to connect to people who can help me to sell $1,000,000 mainframe computer systems.

Ensure that you have three or more contacts in each department/division/company whom you can count on to be your inside salespeople who will look out for you. What do I mean by an *inside salesperson*? While not the decision maker, an inside salesperson might be an influencer who will be consulted during the buying process. They might also be that person who will step into the decision-making role should the current buyer leave or be promoted. Generally, these are folks who like you and like your product and service.

That's rule number 1. This is also a part of discovering a variety of opportunities that may be occurring in different areas of a company at any given time. At the same time, you are protecting yourself should your key contact move on to another position or to a different company. Using tools such as LinkedIn search will assist you in this endeavor.

If you are targeting specific companies, you might try this approach:

1. Go to your target company's websites and find "connect to follow" links for social networks. Follow those and then bookmark them for now, as you will want to return to these networks at a future time.

2. On the company website, find a staff listing if that is available. Quite typically, these will include title, department, phone, and e-mail addresses.

3. Learn to love each network's advanced search! Remember that these searches can also be set to look beyond that of your established network.

4. Use people searches on LinkedIn to find people at specific accounts based on keyword searches pertaining to your target market. You can use "AND" and "OR" syntax as a part of your search when multiple keywords are involved. If you are looking for specific companies, do multiples at one time and then save the search. You can save up to three searches and you will be notified by e-mail of new people matching your search.

5. Find what groups (LinkedIn, Facebook, and Google+) your potential connections belong to, and join those if applicable and allowed. This will allow you to engage prior to connecting, if desired, and will make connecting in the future easier. Also remember that most groups are "connection agnostic". In other words, you can be in the same group and engage with anyone within that group, regardless of whether or not they are even in your extended network.

How else can you expand your network and make it count?

1. Discover the people with whom your connections are speaking. You should be able to identify, evaluate, and connect with those people who are already connected with your connection. This is almost as powerful as a direct introduction!

2. Use each network's search capabilities to target people who have profiles that match your target market. This might be by company, industry, title, or any number of other parameters.

3. Of course, using search to find opportunities based on keywords will uncover connections that you will want to initiate! We will talk more about this a little later.

4. There are several third-party applications (some of which we will discuss in our next chapter) that can assist you in targeting people who are influential. What do we mean by *influential*?

   ➤ They may have many followers and connections

   ➤ While not perfect, applications such as Klout, Kred, and PeerIndex can give us some feeling for an individual's level of social influence

   ➤ They talk about things that we share in common

   ➤ They demonstrate (you can see this on their social streams) a high level of engagement and people are listening and sharing what they share

Connecting with influencers is very powerful! They can not only assist you in amplifying your message, they can also become cheerleaders for your cause. Are you judged by the company you keep? I would think so. If you lie down with dogs, you will get up with fleas. Soar with eagles and you will be flying too! Remember the process! Engage, connect, add to your SCRM, and then manage and nurture your relationships.

Evaluating and grading your contacts

There are several methods that you might use to evaluate the value that a contact brings to your network. As a determination of value, you might ask yourself any combination of these questions:

> ➤ Do they engage with you and are they responsive to your attempts at initiating engagement?

> ➤ How much do they buy?

> ➤ How regularly do they refer you to others?

> ➤ Do they champion your services?

> ➤ Do they share common services and target markets?

Next, we would like to have some way to classify and identify these folks. One way is via tagging. We spoke in an earlier chapter about the "A, B, C" classification method. Your SCRM may have other methods available, including the following:

> ➤ Marking this contact as being "Important".

> ➤ A star-grading system like those used for movies and restaurants. Five stars: valuable. One star: not so valuable.

> ➤ Its own algorithm using keywords that you have specified or it has determined, which will suggest when a contact should be marked as important.

Now that we have graded these folks, what might we want to do next? Set recurring reminders based on their level of importance. Concentrate more on developing closer relationships with these people. Maybe, we add them to a list of group so that we might monitor their activities more closely.

Relationship mapping

Relationship mapping is one of the newer applications that are being developed for social networking. A good example of this can be found on LinkedIn when you visit someone's profile, and you discover that they are a second-degree connection to you. LinkedIn will then identify all of your first-degree connections who are also first-degree connected to this individual. You can then request an introduction. In fact, LinkedIn will also do this with third-degree connections; however, what you will see is that your first-degree connections are connected to "somebody" (their second-degree connection) who is, in turn, connected to your target individual. This is your **map**, and mapping is one of the keys to effectively expanding your network. Facebook, Google+, and Twitter do something similar by identifying shared friends and followers.

The holy grail for relationship mapping will be when all of these network connections are identified and aggregated by one central application. There are vendors who are working on this process. For now, there are steps that you can take to leverage these connections for yourself:

> Be aware that each of the networks provide mapping to at least some degree and take advantage of that. LinkedIn, in particular, will aggressively suggest connections for you.

> Are you connected to each of your team members as well as to other department members within your own company? It's funny that often the last place we think that we need to be connected to is in our own house.

> We've talked about this earlier, but with whom are your connections engaging? They are identifying their relationship map to you.

> Public Twitter lists (those compiled by your connections and even by your competitors) can also be excellent resources for relationship mapping!

> LinkedIn groups (as well as groups and communities on other platforms) provide their own form of *self-mapping*. In other words, groups are generally composed of like-minded individuals who will share common interests and, perhaps, even industries.

Progressive engagement through taps and touches

Would you walk into a crowded business mixer and walk up to someone, hand them your business card, and immediately launch into a pitch to buy your product? Of course not! At least, I would hope not. Instead, you would take the time to get to know this person and to develop your relationship before determining the right time (if there even will be one) to talk about your product or service. You take baby steps, and taps and touches are the social networking versions of these.

Let's say that your goal is to connect with somebody on LinkedIn, but that you do not really know this person. If they are a second- or third-degree connection, you may request an introduction through one of your common first-degree connections. Otherwise, you will send an invitation to connect, which LinkedIn will (hopefully) allow you to personalize. You may also **InMail** (private message) individuals (this is a premium feature but this is available to all LinkedIn accounts including free accounts) or your desired connection may be an OpenLink member who will accept private messages from anybody. Still, your message is likely arriving unannounced and with no previous engagement having occurred.

A better way to maximize your chances to make a formal connection will be through the use of progressive *taps* (one-click pokes) and *touches* (personalized communications). Examples of taps would be retweets and favorites on Twitter, likes and shares on Facebook, likes and endorsements on LinkedIn, and +1s and likes on Google+. Touches would include comments on any of the networks and reply messages on Twitter. Each one of these can and should include that person's name.

For example, what I am seeing a lot lately is people who will engage with me via taps and touches on Twitter and then will follow these activities with a connection request on LinkedIn. Even if that request is not personalized, I generally have some positive memory of our previous engagement, and I am therefore more likely to accept their request.

Groups, particularly on LinkedIn, are great places to progressively engage prior to initiating a connection request. Group settings will allow you to conduct both tap and touch campaigns. Here are some other ways to maximize engagement:

> ➤ What do you know about their likes and interests? Do you have something in common that is not work related? Maybe you can direct them to sources that they might find to be of value.

> ➤ E-mail articles that you think they will find interesting and ask if they know anybody else in their organization who would benefit from these. A good RSS reader such as Feedly will help you with this.

> ➤ Use direct messaging to get past the noise. Everybody's e-mail boxes today are tremendously overloaded, and you can easily get lost in the mass. Group members on LinkedIn can also directly message other group members (regardless of your network degree connection) as long as this is done via the group interface. Additionally, if you share a group with an individual, LinkedIn recognizes this and will pass your request to connect the invitation through without any issue.

> ➤ What is their preferred way to communicate? Use that. Some people like e-mail, while others prefer text messages, one or more of the social networks, or even the phone.

> ➤ What is their preferred social network? Monitor that and pay close attention.

How to build referrals and introductions

Who wants referrals? You do, that's who. Everybody loves referrals and what's not to love about them! Somebody knows somebody else who can potentially use your product or service, and they have advised that person that you are a person who can and will get the job done. The first thing that we have to appreciate about referrals and introductions is that they are **earned** and not given. How do we earn them? We do the following:

> ➤ Develop relationships

> ➤ Promote others before we promote ourselves

> ➤ Perform consistently

Despite rumors to the contrary, bringing donuts to my office every week **does not** earn you anything other than my gratitude for the snacks. Do you want to know what will really get my attention? It's simple. Help me sell more of my stuff, and I will more inclined to help you sell (and I will even buy) more of your stuff! I have pretty strong feelings about this topic, so let's examine it closer.

Earning referrals and introductions can best be accomplished via the consistent application of three general methods.

Method #1 – be awesome!

You have to realize this simple fact: when somebody refers you to one of their good clients or friends, it is their neck that is being potentially placed on the chopping block. If the referral works out great for both parties, they are the heroes, and being seen as such in the eyes of their client is one of the actions that will elevate them from **vendor** to **trusted advisor**. However, if the person who they refer turns out to be a loser, they will be the bigger one. Their status with their client has now been reduced from "vendor" to that of "vendor with a poor judge of character". Ouch!

I'm a funny guy. I keep a mental scorecard on everybody I meet in business as a part of my process to determine whether or not that person is *referral worthy*. The basis for this is my belief that as I interact with you personally, I can expect you to exhibit these same behaviors with anybody I might introduce you to. Why would I think otherwise? So, I am looking for people who:

> ➤ Are consistently professional
> ➤ Are always honest
> ➤ Show that they are responsive
> ➤ Display promptness
> ➤ Treat our business dealings with respect

While I might like you personally, and this is certainly a part of the equation, it's not enough for me to decide whether or not I will be willing to refer you. I may have much to gain from initiating this referral, but the potential risk of this going badly cannot exceed the potential benefits of it going right. Actually, this risk has to be nonexistent. I buy from the same kind of people whom I refer: those whom I like, trust, and respect. So be awesome!

Method #2 – engage with me!

As discussed, if I like, trust, and respect you, the likeliness of my referring you increases. The best way to do this is to make the touches (engage with me). Your overtures must be perceived as being both genuine and thoughtful. Here are some examples of how we can to this socially:

> ➤ Retweet and reply to my updates.
> ➤ Comment and like my posts.
> ➤ Leave comments on my articles.
> ➤ Connect me with somebody whom you think would be valuable to me.
> ➤ Send me an article that you know I will like.
> ➤ While I appreciate your endorsements on LinkedIn, please wait until you feel comfortable enough to write me a recommendation. If you still wish to endorse me, please be sure that it is for an actual skill that I have and not one where I need to look up its definition.

> ➤ My business life is pretty much an open book. I have a lot of folks who reach out to me, and the first question that they ask me is to "tell them a little bit about myself". They probably got my e-mail address from my website. Did they even look at that or maybe even my profile on LinkedIn? No, and it is annoying.

Method # 3 – provide referrals!

One of the best ways to get referrals has always been to give them. *"You scratch my back, and I'll scratch yours."* Does this suggest that we should only perform action "A" in order to receive action "B" in return? Of course not, but providing referrals is a still a powerful tool as is the love of giving referrals for the sheer joy of doing so!

Recently, I have seen a new term being bandied about: *creating social debt*. What is it, how do we create it, and how do we leverage it? Sales Benchmark Index (a great resource) defines it as follows:

> *"Social Debt is the act of doing something of perceived value for an individual. This predisposes them when prompted to "Return the Favor."" When you "Pay It Forward", the receiving person realizes you do something unnecessary. This act creates a "debt" in their mind. Each time you help that person the debt increases. Over time, you then have earned the right to ask. Ask for a referral, introduction to someone, or simply advice."*

 Tip
Be sure to note and record all of your activities into your SCRM!

Next, let's dissect the referral itself. If you wish to receive quality referrals, you will need to also master how to teach others to provide you with quality referrals. What makes a great referral? Please choose one from the following:

1. *"I gave your name to somebody the other day, and they should be calling you."*

2. *"You should call Fred at ABC Company. Please don't use my name, but they may need your product or service."*

3. *"Steve, I spoke with Fred Smith over at ABC Company the other day, and I was telling him about your services. Fred is interested in learning more and is expecting a call from you. He can be reached at 867-5309 and please be sure to use my name."*

It's pretty easy to choose when you see the options in black and white, isn't it? Now that you have been given this great referral, be sure to thank the referrer, let them know that you have followed-up, keep them informed of your progress, and then thank them again! Some folks will reward those who refer them with a gift card or something similar. A friend of mine has a policy to always reward the action, not the result. In other words, just because this referral did not work out, it does not mean that I don't appreciate your efforts! Good policy.

Now, what we need do is to teach others how to give us these same excellent referrals:

> *"Steve, as you know, a large part of my business is based on receiving referrals from great customers like you, and I have really appreciated all of the referrals that you have provided for me! When you do run into somebody to whom you think I could be of help, could you please tell them a bit about me, let them know to expect my call, and then get their contact information to me? In this way, I can be sure to get in touch with them right away and then keep you informed of my progress with them. Thank you!"*

The simple fact is that most *referrals* are not anywhere near as effective as they could be because we don't know how to give them, and our customers have never been taught any differently either. The responsibility for both lies with us.

Trigger events

Ideally, our goal is to turn cold calls into warm calls, and an example of a warm call would be, "*I am contacting this company because I know that they are rapidly adding employees, and this creates a potential need for our services.*" Adding employees and other such company changes are commonly called **trigger events**.

For example, my background was in the electric sign industry. Typical trigger events for me included new construction and businesses moving (relocating or opening). Both would indicate a strong potential for new signage. Prior to social media, how did I uncover these? I drove around, read the paper, and talked to others.

There are a number of ways in which we can leverage the Internet and social media to expose trigger events. For now, let's take a look at Google.

Using Google Search, perform your search based on keywords, but narrow your search to "News". When you perform a Google search based on "News", an option is also given to add this search to Google News just by clicking that selection. I can then go to this dedicated page whenever I like and read the latest news. However, I would like to be notified by e-mail whenever this kind of news is breaking, so I will also create a *Google Alert*.

Next, find out more about specific companies and people that turn up in your alerts by accessing LinkedIn. Note that you could also do a general Google search for these people and businesses and then add the word "LinkedIn" to your search.

Monitoring for opportunities and brand mentions

One of the most powerful features of SCRM is having the capability to monitor the social networks by use of searches and then to convert pertinent results into opportunities that will be managed by your SCRM.

In the following screenshot, I have used my SCRM social dashboard and have searched for "looking for CRM". Please note that at the time of writing this book, LinkedIn no longer offers the ability to search for updates, and Google+ has not yet released this capability to third-party applications.

As you can see, we have a hit. I might engage with this person by offering my assistance. I can also take a closer look at this person's profile and choose to import them as a contact. Let's do that. Next, as depicted in the following screenshot, I will create a task for follow-up and associate this task with this contact record. For that matter, I can also create this task and assign it to another team member or e-mail this update to another party (for example, you are looking for opportunities for one of your clients) for their review.

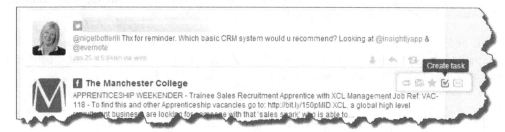

Done! I can now manage this lead from my SCRM, engage as needed with this contact, and then hopefully turn this into an opportunity and then into a sale!

Social support best practices

All of the social best practices that we have discussed so far are equally applicable to your customer support and your marketing departments. However, customer service faces their own unique challenges which can, in turn, either create opportunities for your small business or if not handled correctly, create even bigger headaches. Consider the following (sourced via HubShout— *"Social Media's Impact on Customer Service"*—http://bit. ly/1hDB61W):

> ➤ The social networks are rapidly becoming the vehicle of choice to request customer support.

> ➤ Over 70 percent of customers who have a support issue and express that on social media are expecting a response of some sort from the company within 1 hour. Yes, I said **1 hour**.

> ➤ Over 50 percent of the same customers expect the same level of service on both nights and weekends.

These numbers are huge, and you have an opportunity to be seen as either a hero or as a bum. It will all depend on your response time and your response quality.

Monitoring for brand mentions

One of the best ways to discover customer support opportunities will be to create keyword searches to monitor for your brand name(s) and your product name(s). You will want to create these searches to include every possible variation of both. Also remember that when your keyword is preceded by a # (hash tag) on Twitter, that term becomes searchable. For example, if your company name is BigService, #BigService is a searchable term all on its own.

You will respond via the same social channel that originated the request, determine the nature of the request, and create a support case if applicable. Next, follow your established process to complete each support case record and to follow that through to its completion.

Tip

Responding to customer needs and questions

There will be times when people will request information about your company. This may be directed at the company itself, or more often, it is one person who asks their friends for their recommendations or how their experience has been with a particular product or service. Either way, you must be prepared to respond and to offer your assistance!

Create dedicated accounts, pages, and sites

Many smart companies are creating dedicated Twitter accounts as well as specific pages (or page tabs) on Facebook and Google+ that are devoted to customer support, and they will heavily promote these services. Not only are they demonstrating their commitment to support via social media, many small businesses will find this to be extremely cost effective when compared to call centers or other *brick and mortar* operations.

Web-based support sites are also important. In our next chapter, we will be discussing some third-party customer-facing applications that can not only assist you in these duties but can also provide great on-line and even self-serve resources for your valued and potential customers.

Social marketing best practices

You may find that there is quite a bit of crossover between customer support and marketing. For example, it remains the responsibility of both to monitor the social networks for your brand/product mentions, for new opportunities, and to respond to the needs and questions of your customers. However, as a member of your marketing department, your responsibilities will go quite a bit beyond that.

Social media campaigns

Assuming that you have been charged with creating buzz for your small business via social media campaigns, you are actively encouraging others to engage with your business on these same channels. You are looking for shares, comments, retweets, replies, likes, and +1s. When you receive those, and you will, it is critical that you be prepared to respond in kind with a thank you, a follow-up question, or whatever it takes to drive the conversation and the relationship forward. If you find you have an interest in your company's services, create a task for sales and have them move this to their SCRM for immediate follow through.

Directing others to your web pages

Your company's web pages should be your #1 (although not yours alone) resource for content sharing. When you share a link to one of your pages, that link is disseminated and amplified throughout the social networks. You may share three (or more) different types of pages:

> ➤ Static pages that tell folks more about your company

> ➤ Articles that you have written about your product or service and maybe even tips on how to use those better

> ➤ Landing pages with an effective CTA (call-to-action)

We will talk about landing pages and CTAs in the next chapter, but this is where you will be directing people to an offer—most often free—in return for their contact information. These people have taken the first step toward becoming active leads in your SCRM.

Creating and maintaining customer communities

Groups and pages that can be found on LinkedIn, Facebook, and Google+ are your domains! It is your responsibility to do the following:

> - Encourage readers to follow or join.
> - Create and promote lively discussions.
> - Generate excitement with polls, games, and contests.
> - Maintain an atmosphere that is inviting.
> - Provide great free advice regarding the best uses of your product or service and of other products that you think would be of value to your audience.
> - Ask your visitors for their assistance. This creates brand buy-in!
> - Be active and responsive! There is absolutely nothing worse than sites like these that either appear to be a ghost town or where people who want to talk to you remain talking to themselves. In fact, these actions will create more damage than good.

These communities create a feeling of belonging for your customers and a sense of being a part of your team. Always remember that these people have voluntarily opted in to your message, and this is hugely important! As part of your team, they now become some of your staunchest brand advocates and ambassadors! Of course, your goal remains to move these people to your SCRM, nurture relationships, and convert fans into customers.

Summary

We have just finished a critical chapter. It is time for you to refocus on your goals and ensure that you and your staff are properly prepared to leverage the social aspects of Social CRM. This means, if you have not yet done this, get your social accounts created and your social profiles looking good!

As a review, SCRM has the potential to take your data files (records) and turn those into relationships that will provide you with a revenue return. You can follow this simple process:

1. Listening.
2. Engaging to discover opportunities.
3. Establishing a more formal connection.
4. Moving these contacts and engagements to your SCRM by creating the appropriate record(s)
5. Manage them going forward from this platform.

If you follow this process, you will see results! It's not that complicated. It's what you should already be doing in your day-to-day business activities.

The next chapter will explore some of the ways that you might increase the effectiveness of your SCRM through the implementation of third-party applications.

8

Enhancing Your Social CRM with Third-party Applications and Integrations

We now begin our discussion of how you might increase the capabilities of your SCRM via the deployment of third-party applications (apps) and integrations. In this chapter, we will cover the following points:

> ➤ There may be an SCRM for your industry
> ➤ Integration overview
> ➤ Integrations 101
> ➤ Office applications
> ➤ Sales applications
> ➤ Customer support applications
> ➤ Marketing applications

While we have touched on this many times before, always remember that regardless of where and how you generate social activities, these social conversations should feed back to your SCRM where they will be aggregated in created contact (or other) records. Exactly how this works will depend entirely on the capabilities of your chosen SCRM.

Before we discuss third-party integrations, we should talk about the potential that an SCRM or SCRM package may have already been designed for your specific industry.

There may be an SCRM for your industry

It is not unusual, particularly for those industries that seem to have specialized (but still standardized) needs and a large number of potential users, for companies to develop SCRM applications for that specific industry. This might be:

> ➤ A program built from the ground up

> ➤ An SCRM that is available from the vendor that has been preconfigured for a specific industry(s)

> ➤ A package offered by a value-added reseller who has done this same preconfiguration and has additionally combined the SCRM with specific third-party applications in order to enhance its features

While such a specialized SCRM may be available, you will still wish to vet it completely in order to ensure that it will meet all of your needs.

Integration overview

Many SCRMs today are as much platforms as they are systems. This means that you can integrate them with many third-party offerings (from other vendors) in order to expand and enhance their capabilities. Think about it this way: if you wished to use data found in your SCRM in another application, which would be an integration opportunity, or if there are sales, customer support, or marketing functions that are not adequately addressed by your SCRM, there may be an available integration to facilitate this.

This chapter will expose you to some ideas by concentrating on common and popular deployments. However, before we do that, let's take a look at how these unions might actually work:

1. **Throw it over the fence**: This is the simplest form of integration where you can gather a group of records and then *throw* that data (export it) to another program. Typically, the data that you are exporting will be preconfigured to match the data format that is required by the other application.

2. **One-way syncing**: The data will either sync from your SCRM to the other application (automatically), or it will sync from the other application to your SCRM, but it will not do this both ways.

3. **Two-way syncing**: Data syncs both ways between your SCRM and the other program.

Let me give you an example of all three options with an e-mail newsletter program:

1. I manually create a group of records on my SCRM and export those to my newsletter program where they are automatically added to my mailing list. As I have performed this function manually, this equates to *throwing the data over the fence*, and no actual syncing takes place.

2. Every time I create a record and tag it *newsletter*, that record is automatically added to my newsletter mailing list. However, whenever I send out a newsletter, a note registering this action is not added to the appropriate contact records. This is a one-way sync from your SCRM to the newsletter program.

3. Using example 2, in addition to syncing records to my mailing list, when a newsletter now is sent out, that activity is also automatically added to my contact records. The syncing is two way.

For obvious reasons, two-way syncing is the preferable choice. If there is a lesson to be learned here, it is to **do your homework!** When a vendor tells you that there is an integration available, ask hard questions in order to determine what that means to them and what that will ultimately mean to you!

Also, be advised that integrations with other programs will likely require that you establish a separate account with that application and that there may be additional fees (monthly or one-time) that are associated with that service.

Make a note

In this section, I will share some names of common applications (my apologies if you were left out!). Please be cautioned that my doing so is in no way an endorsement of any program nor any sort of a guarantee that they will even be in business tomorrow. I am making no representation that they will be suitable for your small-business purposes. For that matter, your final SCRM choice may offer either limited or no integration options at all. With the exception of being a solution partner for Nimble SCRM and Hootsuite, I have absolutely no affiliation with any of the applications that I will mention.

This is a rapidly moving and evolving marketplace, and companies do come and they do go. The good news is if there is a valid requirement for something to perform this particular function, there will generally be more than one good option to choose from, and there will always be new applications that are being introduced to occupy that space.

Integrations 101

It's a good idea that we first discuss some fundamentals, as there are many methods and variables that will affect how vendors will ultimately be able to offer these services.

Application Programming Interface

Wikipedia defines API as, "In computer programming, an application programming interface (API) specifies how some software components should interact with each other". For our purposes, an *API* is coding that is provided by one vendor application (for example, LinkedIn) that can be used by another vendor's program (for example, your SCRM) in order to create the connection that will allow the two different software components (LinkedIn and your SCRM) to interact with each other.

An API might provide access points to some parts of that program but not to other parts. In the case of LinkedIn, at present, it will allow other programs to see your first-degree connections but not your second and third-degree connections.

Your SCRM will also provide its own API for third-party vendors who wish to offer integrations to your SCRM application, and your SCRM may allow this third-party vendor access to certain records types within the system but will not grant this same access to other record types. For example, they might be able to see and use contact records but not opportunity records.

If you ever find yourself wondering *"why can I do this but not that?"*, there is a good chance that an API limitation (by one or both parties) may be to blame.

Your SCRM provides the integration

Your SCRM vendor may create integrations of their own, such as widgets for your e-mail or for a social dashboard. Realizing that third-party apps make their SCRM much more valuable, many vendors will also provide a dedicated portal for you to review and shop for available integrations. These are generally referred to as *"Marketplaces"*. A simple search for *"Vendor Name Application Marketplace"* should disclose whether one exists.

E-mail-based SCRM

There is also another class of SCRM, often with very limited capabilities, that will actually use your e-mail platform (generally, Gmail or Google Apps) as the foundation for the SCRM itself. These can be functional for smaller businesses with one or two users. The most common source for these will be through the Google Chrome Marketplace, which allows you to add extensions and apps to your Chrome browser. Access these via your Chrome browser settings under tools, and then search for "CRM".

Gadgets, plugins, and extensions

While vendors might call them different things, gadgets, widgets, and plugins are all mini-services that are used to connect your SCRM to other frequently used applications, and the majority of these will be found where many of us spend a great deal of time: in your e-mail inbox. You will find frequent offerings for Outlook and Gmail (or Google Apps). While Google products are standardized, you will need to verify Gmail or Google Apps compatibility with your own SCRM system.

Here is an example of my SCRM widget for Gmail (bottom section of the image).

Outlook can be a bit tricky. While an application may be available to bring your SCRM into Outlook as a plugin, it might only work with Windows and not with Mac, or vice versa. Outlook 365 (cloud-based) might use a different widget, or it may be available as a browser extension. Browser extensions can be found for both Chrome and Firefox (Firefox calls them add-ons) as well as for Safari and Internet Explorer.

These little apps can also be used to connect your SCRM to your social dashboards as well as other programs. Typically, they will allow you to view that person's contact record as it appears in your SCRM. It may also provide an interface to add a record to your SCRM where none is present and maybe even to add notes and tasks to your SCRM contact record without ever having to leave and go to the SCRM itself.

Another increasingly popular way that SCRMs allow additional features is with the use of iFrames. iFrames allow you to display an external web page from within a different application. For example, my SCRM will allow me to display a Bing search or map of that specific client and their specific address based on the information that Bing finds in my contact record. The SCRM has created a dedicated tab for this use. However, not all web pages can be displayed as an iFrame, and they may not have the capability to search your contact record for the information that it needs in order to correctly display the pertinent information.

Signature lines and social widgets for e-mails

Custom signature lines can be used to direct people to your website and to your social networks, to display images, or even to feature your latest blog post. Remember the Social Media Ecosystem and how this ties back into your SCRM. For Gmail and some other platforms, look at WiseStamp and BrandMyMail. Outlook has built-in HTML (Hyper Text Markup Language) signature capability. My WiseStamp signature is shown on the left-hand side of the following figure.

Social widgets can also be added to your e-mail, and these can serve two purposes. Rapportive, shown on the right-hand side, is now owned by LinkedIn and, effective July 31, 2014, went through some changes to provide a deeper integration with that network.

Connecting apps

There is a whole separate category for services that are actually used to function as an intermediary between your SCRM and another application. In essence, these perform a handshake between the two, and they are usually used when no other formal integration is available. Tasks that they may perform include the following:

> The importing of records from one program to another

> Record syncing and/or updating between two applications

> Connecting one program to another

These apps have become very powerful and quite easy to use. They are also becoming what I like to call the *fine print* of the application integration world. It is very common to find an available integration to a desirable service, and when reading the *fine print*, you will discover that the union is accomplished via a connecting app (also called data connectors). This is neither good nor bad, but it is something that you should be aware of to understand the potential limitations.

So, with connecting apps, you are now using three applications. Your connecting app will be used as the intermediary in order to "join" your SCRM to your chosen third-party application. A few of the common apps of this nature include the following:

> ➤ Zapier to connect and automate actions between applications.

> ➤ Cazoomi SyncApps will allow you to sync certain records and fields between cloud-based applications

> ➤ IFTTT (If This, Then That), which triggers one action when another occurs.

> ➤ itDuzzit, which connects cloud-based programs.

> ➤ Import2, which facilitates the import of data between applications.

> ➤ PieSync is a relatively new application that facilitates complete data syncing between cloud-based applications. While this may sound like a simple application, it can be incredibly complex, and PieSync is doing a very nice job!

In general, connecting apps are very good to perform common utility functions such as transferring records from one app to another. They will generally perform simple tasks only and they will complete these tasks quite efficiently.

Combining SCRM programs

This may seem like an odd marriage, but in many cases, this will work quite well. I have a CRM "A," but that CRM does not have social networking features, whereas SCRM "B" does. However SCRM "B" may be strong in social networking, but it is weak in terms of contact records. So, I create a window to integrate that SCRM's social data into my existing CRM, and now I have a more fully featured SCRM.

It's done completely separately from your SCRM

Even if your SCRM is highly social, there are always going to be applications that will focus on a specific task, which will offer a more developed feature set for that task only. As they are concentrating on one aspect only, their capabilities in this area will likely be in excess of that found on your SCRM, which addresses a wider variety of tasks.

A good social dashboard that allows you to monitor and manage multiple social networks may be the best example. Hootsuite, TweetDeck, and Sprout Social are three popular examples of dedicated platforms that may be more efficient in this specific operation than your own SCRM. Activities that you conduct from within them will still come back to SCRM.

The same could probably be said of lead-generation programs and some customer service and marketing applications as well. Unfortunately, you may discover that no integration with your SCRM is available on any level. My advice: *do not get caught up in the trap that your SCRM must fully integrate with everything in order to be effective.* Your SCRM is a specific tool that is designed to address certain tasks that will, in turn, increase your small business revenues, and you can still employ other standalone apps that will *also* increase your revenues with or without having an integration.

Your SCRM will probably not come equipped to handle your front-office applications such as accounting. However, there are many solutions available, particularly for the most popular programs such as cloud-based QuickBooks. If nothing else, connecting apps such as Zapier may be able to provide some basic level of integration.

Accounting

There is certainly a strong case to be made to integrate your SCRM with accounting:

> ➤ A contact is created in your SCRM, and when appropriate, it is easily added as a customer to your accounting system

> ➤ When an estimate is created, it is automatically assigned and attached to the appropriate contact or account record in your SCRM and a proposal/quote is generated based on that data

> ➤ When an opportunity is sold (converted), that information is sent to your accounting package for work-order processing, eventual invoicing, and the commission on that sale is calculated and added to the payroll

> ➤ Costs incurred as part of a marketing campaign are added to the appropriate accounting categories, including accounts payable

> ➤ Warranty work or customer service work orders generated by customer support are automatically sent to accounting to be appropriately handled

Will your choice of SCRM integrate with your existing accounting system? Maybe. Will it integrate as tightly as the examples shown above? Not likely, but it is not impossible. If your CRM has SharePoint capabilities (this is a Microsoft product and is found with Microsoft Dynamics CRM), being able to integrate this task (and other workflows) may be substantially easier.

However, if you are in an industry where there are strong players who provide industry-specific accounting software, there is a possibility that they may have already researched and provided some sort of SCRM functionality. They might offer an optional module or might have taken the steps necessary to fully integrate with one or more specific SCRM offerings.

Project management

Project management, and to a large degree team collaboration, can be a popular SCRM application. In fact, some SCRM/CRMs will have project management either built in or will offer this capability as an optional module. If having project management integration with your SCRM is important to you, you might look at Asana and Podio.

Meetings

TimeTrade is one app (there are others) that will allow you to block out times that people can then choose from in order to schedule a meeting with you. This can go a long way toward eliminating the constant e-mail back and forth that occurs when trying to coordinate meetings.

The best way to promote this is to add a link to your e-mail signature line or as a clearly visible button on your website. You are notified of these meetings, and they are automatically added to your calendar. Multiple appointment types are available, and this app can cover from the very simple to the very complex scheduling needs and will integrate (at least) with Salesforce.

Online meetings, such as those that are conducted via GoToMeeting and WebEx, also have the potential to be joined with SCRM.

Outbound calling

Outbound calling may be a function of a marketing automation application, and this will be discussed later in this chapter. However, simply placing a call to a contact from within the confines of that contact record may be facilitated through the use of a couple of simple services such as Google Voice or Skype.

Sales applications

There are simply tons of third-party programs that are available for sales, and there is literally no way to address them all in this book. If you have a need, a simple search will likely bring up a bevy of options. Many of these, particularly when combined with SCRM, are designed to help you better leverage the social networks.

Tip

This is a rapidly evolving area with a **great number** of vendors who are both coming and going. You will want to try any application before making any sort of investment. Some may be well designed for B2B companies, while others may be best for B2C only. Most (not all), at this time, are focused on Twitter, and your target market might or might not be best engaged on this network.

Contact targeting and lead discovery

There tends to be an overlap between these two areas with many applications that are available doing both. When you think about it, targeting people who will buy or influence others to buy your product is not that much different from finding people who are expressing a specific need for your services.

Twitter seems to be the common network that is being addressed by these services, largely due to its wide-open architecture. Facebook may be available for some and LinkedIn for others, although at the time of writing this book, LinkedIn had recently removed the ability to search for individual updates (formerly known as LinkedIn Signals). Google+ is still largely a closed system to third-party applications.

There are general tools, such as social dashboards, that will allow you to search for user profiles based on keywords that match your target audience and will also allow you to discover social updates that express a potential need for the services that you offer. We have previously mentioned both Hootsuite and Sprout Social as potential solutions that will provide you with this functionality.

However, there are also much more sophisticated and specialized tools available, and many of these will integrate with a variety of SCRMs. You can also use them to discover and engage with relationships and opportunities and then add them to your SCRM. In some cases, these applications feature quite advanced algorithms that are used to determine sentiment (hate, like, love, want, and so on), Boolean (AND, OR), "do not include X", influence scores (Klout, Kred, PeerIndex), and other formulas in order to determine the best possible matches for your search. Some that may be worthy of your consideration are as follows:

- SocialBro
- MarketMeSuite
- Twtrland
- LeadSift
- Leadfindr
- Little Bird
- Socedo
- SalesLoft

Even better, many of these services are based on the freemium model, meaning that there are both free and (if needed) paid versions. All have free trials.

Relationship mapping and customer intelligence

We spoke a little bit about relationship mapping in our previous chapter. If the purpose of connecting with others on the social networks is to leverage those connections in order to develop new profitable connections, then relationship mapping may be the Holy Grail. These capabilities are relatively new, but they are rapidly evolving.

A number of new applications are cropping up to address this specific task in a variety of ways.

- KiteDesk
- InsideView
- Data.com
- OFunnel

Even better, particularly when integrated with a small business SCRM, in some cases, these programs will allow you to create contact and lead records on the fly.

Document preparation and delivery

Having the ability to create form letters based on templates is not an uncommon SCRM feature nor is some sort of mail merge with Word. This might also include the use of templates for e-mail blasts (marketing). However, there are other third-party applications available that will assist you in more sophisticated document-preparation tasks. For example, proposal (quote) creation in conjunction with SCRM is available. These may allow you to:

- Create a document library that includes your commonly used forms and marketing collateral
- Assemble and personalize your proposal by pulling docs from this library and then merging those with contact information that is found in your SCRM records
- Add media such as slide shows and video to your proposal
- Deliver these proposals via e-mail
- Track dates and times for e-mail opening, for each page reviewed on the proposal, and for links that are found in your proposal that have been clicked
- Know if and when your proposal was shared with somebody inside or outside of an organization
- Provide a convenient online document-signing routine

This is powerful stuff! You might look at QuoteRoller and edocr as two such applications.

Pipeline management

The majority of SCRMs will include some level of pipeline/opportunity management. However, you may want or need a more sophisticated solution. Pipeline management is an excellent example of how third-party integrations can meet those requirements. Pipedrive is one such program, and for some people, Pipedrive can also perform adequately as a standalone CRM.

Certainly, your sales department is not the only area of your company that will benefit from your SCRM investment. Customer support and sales work hand in hand in your small business' concentrated effort to exceed customer expectation which, in turn, leads to more sales. There are many third-party integrations for customer support as well!

Customer support applications

Is having the ability to deliver customer support via the Internet, including social media, important to you? There are many support-specific programs available that will integrate (in some manner) with a number of popular SCRMs.

The fact is, even if a small business SCRM has customer-support functions, it will probably not do those very well, and what it will do in this area will be very limited. By the same token, customer-support applications that tout an integrated SCRM may not perform these SCRM functions anywhere near as completely as a dedicated SCRM will. Each specializes in a different core functionality.

Web-based support sites

Web-based support sites can offer your small business customers a number of services, and if a specific account or contact is found on your SCRM, it should also update tickets to their records:

FAQ: A frequently asked questions page or a shared wiki is a great way to address those questions which arise with frequency. As discussed earlier, people want immediate answers to their questions, and if they can do this self-serve without the need to create a support ticket, they and you both win! Common elements that might be included in an FAQ section would be:

> **Help desks**: This aspect of customer support will include the ability for your customer to create help tickets and for you to respond to and manage these tickets.

> **Education**: How-to articles and how-to videos are always popular, and once again, can save you tons of money by minimizing the need for direct support.

> **Support blog**: Having a dedicated support blog is a great way to announce new features and also to advise your customers of planned maintenance or other outages (if that is applicable to your small business).

> **Communities**: Creating and then monitoring a customer community where your users can assist each other is a really great idea! There is that sense of everyone belonging to the team. However, I cannot begin to count the number of times that I have visited such communities only to find frustration and despair, because the vendor has adopted the attitude that "Hey, now I don't have to deal with this. They can take care of themselves." Now, what you find is customers who are flailing around, looking for help from you, and you are nowhere to be found. You are not creating brand ambassadors. You are creating brand detractors. Tragic!

> ➤ **Feature requests**: Allowing customers to make feature requests and even giving them the ability to vote requests up or down is a great way to leverage crowd sourcing! With crowd sourcing, everybody is given the opportunity to help determine the direction of your services, making them feel empowered and that they are a member of your team.

Social monitoring and sentiment analysis

With social media becoming an increasingly popular place for people to initiate support requests and product questions, many of these dedicated programs can be configured to monitor the social networks, evaluate the update based on both sentiment (like; hate) and urgency (911!; "I wish it did ..."), and then to automatically create support tickets and assign those to representatives for follow-up.

Some popular programs that may be worthy of your consideration are as follows:

> ➤ UserVoice
> ➤ Get Satisfaction
> ➤ Desk.com
> ➤ Zendesk

These are all very good programs, and depending on the size of your organization (they are generally priced based on your number of support agents) and on your specific needs, they are surprisingly affordable and a great investment (with a high potential ROI) for any company with this type of need.

Marketing applications

SCRM and marketing automation can be the perfect match and for exactly the same reason that customer support is another very popular SCRM integration. If this is an important aspect of your small business, it makes sense to invest in the tools needed to do it correctly.

Marketing automation and integration

What can you expect from marketing automation and its integration into your SCRM?

> ➤ Website development and maintenance, including landing pages, calls to action, blogging, website analytics, and search engine optimization
> ➤ E-mail marketing including drip e-mails where emails are sent on a preset schedule to parties who have shown an interest in your services
> ➤ Lead-capturing and scoring including sending these to the drip-e-mail system while simultaneously distributing the leads to outbound callers for immediate follow-up

You can also probably expect extensive training and support as well as a subscription fee that will likely dwarf your monthly small business SCRM investment. Plan on spending several hundreds of dollars per month, as a starting point. As a small business, this may or not be cost effective for you. However, if your business model is heavily based on online sales or you deal with high-ticket items, it could be worth a look. Some well-known vendors include the following:

- Act-On
- HubSpot
- Infusionsoft
- Marketo
- Eloqua

Marketing automation on a budget

If you like the idea of marketing automation but need to do so on a limited budget, there are some low-cost alternatives such as ToutApp and Okotopost, although none will be anywhere close in sophistication as will a dedicated automation application. Web-to-lead and e-mail marketing are two such examples, and both, particularly when used in combination with each other as well as with your SCRM, can be quite effective!

Web-to-lead

Web-to-lead is a very common task and is generally quite easy to configure. I use a freemium (the free version of an otherwise fee-based application) program called Wufoo, which allows me to create contact forms on my website, and when someone fills in the contact information, a contact record is automatically created in my SCRM and given the tag *lead*. I have also connected this form to my MailChimp newsletter account, and the individual is given the option to opt-in to my monthly newsletter. In this example, both my SCRM and my newsletter application are connected to my web form program.

Contact forms generally work best when there is something of value that you are offering that person and that something is generally free. For example, you might offer a free e-book or a free webinar. Offerings of this nature are generally showcased in what is referred to as a *call-to-action* box, which will attractively present your offer and encourage others to take advantage of it. My CTA boxes connect to my newsletter program that also facilitates the delivery of a free pdf document.

E-mail marketing

Newsletters and other announcements such as events are another very common application and those that are popular seem to pop up just about everywhere on the integration map. Once again, you will wish to clarify what your SCRM's definition of *integration* really is. For example, it should be easy to conduct a search on your SCRM to arrive at a group of records that you can export to your newsletter program and maybe, even being able to create a segment (a subgroup of your e-mail mailing list for your newsletters). A more desirable solution might be a little more elaborate:

> ➤ Whenever an e-mail is generated by the newsletter, a note is added to that contact record (time and date stamped) that indicates that this collateral was sent out.

> ➤ A tab is created within your SCRM records that is dedicated to this integration and will also provide you with data for both individual addressees (as well as for your entire campaign). It will track:

>> ➤ Whether or not each e-mail was opened

>> ➤ Clicks on links found in the piece

>> ➤ A history of your interaction with this individual or account

Some of these applications will also provide for drip e-mail and other limited marketing automation functions. Drip e-mails are generally a series of template, although personalized, e-mails that are delivered automatically on a set schedule, based on a customer's specific product interests. These are used to continue to build interest in that product and to ultimately convert this customer into making a purchase decision. Take a look at these:

> ➤ Constant Contact
> ➤ iContact
> ➤ AWeber
> ➤ MailChimp

E-mail marketing is recognized as an extremely powerful weapon in your arsenal! The reason for this is actually pretty simple. People on your e-mail list have opted-in to your message. In other words, they are asking you to keep them informed of what is going on in your business. This is more powerful than any "like" on any social network. Your job is to keep them on your list!

Summary

In this chapter, we explored some of the third-party applications that may be used to expand and enhance the capabilities of your SCRM. Key points to remember:

> ➤ Not every third-party program will integrate with every SCRM.

> ➤ A third-party application may provide you with valuable benefits even if it does not integrate or fully integrate, with your SCRM. Do not rule these applications out!

> ➤ What constitutes *"integration"* will vary from app to app and might further vary from SCRM to SCRM, so do your homework in order to avoid not having your expectations met!

In our next (and final) chapter, we will be reviewing the important points that we have covered in the previous chapters. We will discuss the day-to-day maintenance of your SCRM. Finally, we will wrap things up by exploring how to evaluate your return on investment in order to ensure that you are receiving the maximum returns that are possible.

9

Managing Your SCRM and Evaluating Your Investment

We have come to the end of our journey. In this chapter, we would first like to provide you with a quick review of some of the key points that we have discussed in our previous topics. This chapter will wrap things up with the following topics:

➤ Managing your SCRM

➤ Evaluating the effectiveness of the system

Let's get started!

Managing your SCRM

Much of what you will do regarding the management of your SCRM will be based upon establishing and understanding certain criteria:

1. Who will be responsible for managing the system? Will there be multiple people, each of whom is in charge of a specific task(s), or will it be one person who is in charge of all tasks?
2. What activities will be managed and on what schedule will these be performed?
3. How is each task to be completed?

The last item may be the most important. You will need to learn how to perform each of these tasks, and a part of this is knowing what to expect every time you do so. You will want to test and then adjust every procedure prior to establishing a consistent process for its implementation.

Understanding user issues

A critical place to begin your evaluation will be with your users themselves. What is their perception of the system? Are they having any challenges in using the system? What results, positive or negative, are they seeing? What can we do, and what should we do, to make this better for all of us, including our customers?

Being able to maximize the ROI potential of your SCRM will be dependent to a large extent on your users actually using it and doing so consistently. Why would anybody not use something that you have spent so much time and money on, for which you have gone to great lengths to involve them in the decision-making process, and where you have provided top-rated training? Try human nature!

We are all naturally uncomfortable with learning new behaviors. In fact, we are often so uncomfortable that we will abandon the experience rather than continue the unpleasant exercise. Remember these four words: *training, reinforcement, accountability*, and *patience*.

We provide the support and training that is needed as people are learning. We reinforce their positive behaviors. We hold them accountable for following through. We show patience as they adjust and adapt. Make liberal use of all four!

It is critical that you stay on top of and address any challenges prior to them careening out of control. One of the more effective ways to do this is via the use of reporting. If you receive daily reports that reflect your team's activities, meetings, and forecasts, and your team is getting these same reports, any discrepancies should be readily apparent to all (such reports may be a part of your SCRM dashboard).

If you do identify areas in need of improvement, the question now becomes, "Why?" Is it because of the following reasons:

➤ Training? Do your people really know how to use the system correctly?

➤ Is there a procedural misunderstanding? We are learning a lot of new routines and new processes. Is everyone clear on how these are to be completed?

There's no need to panic if you address these issues as they occur. These are all normal parts of the *settling in process* and they are to be expected.

Watching out for common challenges

Salespeople, in particular (I can say this because I am one), are notorious for cutting paperwork corners. Part of this is caused by their go-go mentality. Another piece of this may be their natural aversion to routine tasks. Regardless of department and responsibilities, look at the following and, in each case, *think back to the four words*:

> ➤ **Look at individual records** (account, contact, opportunity, lead, support case, campaign): Do you like what you see? Do the records appear to be complete and up-to-date? If they do not, one of two things may be occurring. Either the records are not being updated (or even created) correctly or in a timely manner, or this is an accurate reflection of accounts not being serviced and called on correctly. Neither of these is good.

> ➤ **Users are not adding appointments, activities, and tasks**: This is very common. While someone may be very good at creating records, they might not be equally efficient at registering activities that relate to these records. This presents a problem. A record that does not reflect activities, social or otherwise, is nothing more than a business card, and this defeats the entire purpose of having an SCRM to begin with.

> ➤ **Users are not completing appointments and tasks**: Actually, they are either not completing them or they are not taking the time to convert the status of each to *having been completed*.

> ➤ **Their pipeline (or the equivalent customer support or marketing report) has not changed in weeks**: Once again, is this reflective of the status of these records not being consistently updated, or are these opportunities stuck and not going anywhere? The latter is not an SCRM issue, but rather a sales/support/marketing training challenge.

On the other hand, it is also not uncommon for salespeople to neglect to update these records as their status (value, stage, percentage chance of closing, anticipated close date, and even final resolution) changes and/or to do so in a timely fashion. Of course, this not being done will render your entire forecast useless.

What if it is a system problem?

There is a chance it's not a user behavior problem at all, but one of a number of potential system issues. Your challenges might be caused by an improper system configuration; something in your initial setup or some other aspect, for example; otherwise, it could be a system bug. System bugs (temporary or otherwise) will likely be more common in cloud-based systems due to the fact that they are generally being updated with new features on a fairly regular basis. Add a new feature; break something else! If you have created custom reports and don't like what you see, are you 100 percent certain that the data you have requested is even being pulled from the system properly?

The answer to any of these scenarios is to do your homework, research the issue on your vendor support site and, if necessary, seek outside help or file a support ticket. Nothing works 100 percent accurately 100 percent of the time. Still, your trouble-free uptime should be well in excess of 95 percent. Otherwise, you may be forced to consider your options, and that might include moving to a different system. However, if you properly performed your due diligence in your SCRM selection process, taking this drastic step would be a highly unusual scenario.

Day-to-day management of your system

There are many important tasks that will be related to the day-to-day management of your SCRM. Anticipate each and establish guidelines and time tables for their proper completion.

Adding and deleting users

From time-to-time, you will be required to add or delete users. First, who will be responsible for this? Next, develop a routine and a checklist. For example:

> ➤ What should be done when we add a new user?
> ➤ Make sure that any records that are associated with a deleted user will not also be deleted.
> ➤ What about e-mails that are associated with a user who is being deleted? We will want those to continue to be a part of their associated SCRM records. For that matter, what happens when we delete that user's e-mail address?
> ➤ What will you do with active accounts, deals, and cases? You will want to assign these to another user. What are the procedures for doing this?

I don't have universal answers to these questions; however, your chosen SCRM will certainly have guidelines pertaining to these actions. Make sure that you review and test prior to proceeding. Finally, remember to change all login names and associated passwords for deleted users, and you should also ensure that this user did not have permissions to override these changes on their own.

Importing new lists and updating existing lists

From time to time, you may find the need to import new lists of customers, or leads, to your SCRM. These may be lists that you have purchased. Review *Chapter 5, Choosing and Implementing Your New Social CRM*. Be sure to import these lists to their proper destination records. In other words, are they leads, opportunities, contacts, accounts, cases, or campaigns?

There may also be times when you will re-import your existing contact lists in order to add new records or update existing ones. For example, my SCRM will not, at this time, sync contact records. For a variety of reasons, before I started using PieSync, I chose to create new contact records in Google and then to export those, weekly, to my SCRM. In the largest majority of cases, this is a seamless and trouble-free operation; however, there will always be challenges, and one of the most frequent of these is duplicate records.

Problems with duplicates

Duplicate records are the bane of every SCRM, and they are, unfortunately, inevitable. If not a duplicate record, you may have duplicate information fields on any given record. Addresses are one common area that seem to be susceptible to duplication.

What can you do to minimize this issue? The best thing that you can do is ensure that you are starting with a clean list. A clean list is devoid of typos and misspellings. The social networks can exacerbate this issue as we now have those profiles to contend with as well.

But, you will still have duplicates regardless, and you will need to perform the following actions:

> ➤ Edit individual records to eliminate duplicate field entries
> ➤ Find and merge duplicate records

Finding and merging duplicate records (combining two or more records into one) will involve a bit of testing and evaluation. Your SCRM may only offer a record by record search for duplicates. In other words, from a given record, I will ask the SCRM to find potential duplicates.

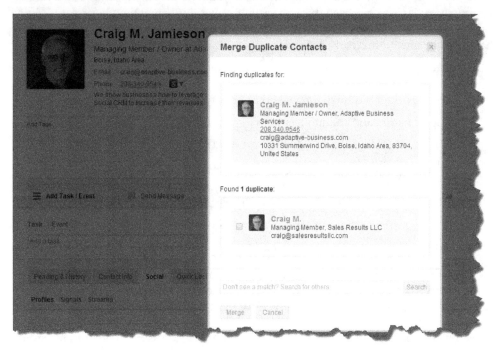

Without even looking at the full records, you should be able to easily determine in the previous image exactly why there are duplicate records. Both are me, but nothing matches: name, title, company name, or email address. Yet, both are accurate (I have two business names) and they both happen to be duplicates.

You may be able to select specific records from a list and ask that these records be merged. Your SCRM may also include a master one-click solution (scan all records) to find duplicates and merge them, although even this one-click method should allow you to selectively choose whether or not to merge any given set of records.

You will need to determine how your SCRM will weigh these records. In other words, given two records, which is the dominant record (the most complete and accurate) into which you wish to merge the additional information from the other? Every application I have seen seems to treat this activity differently.

If you start with record A and then ask to merge it with record B, record A may be treated as the main record or it may be the other way around. The first record that you check from a list may be the dominant record, and then again it may not. You will need to test this for yourself.

Report management

What reports would you like to see (and who else should see them?), how often do you wish to generate them, and what data do you require each to contain? What I have found to be true, though this is only applicable if you have the capability of modifying or creating them, is that reports go through various stages until an optimum format is settled upon. Even then, you will generally repeat this process at a later date as your needs either change or become more clearly defined.

Report creation generally includes a large number of options, including the following:

> The report format, including whether or not to display charts or graphs
> Report names and column headings
> What data (fields) are included in the report
> Filters to pull only certain information, or to ignore other data, based on Boolean searches
> How to group data items (by person, by case, by team, and so on)
> Totals, or some other calculation, by columns
> When and how to generate the report

In other words, there are a lot of options, which means that you have just as many opportunities to configure something incorrectly or to forget to choose to add important data. For that matter, you may find that you have not yet configured a field to contain the data that you wish to display. Reports are absolutely one of the most valuable features of any small business SCRM. Be prepared to invest the time necessary in order to receive the maximum value from yours.

Evaluating system effectiveness

The one thing that everybody wants to know about, and wants to talk about, is ROI. How will I know that I am receiving an adequate return on my investment? I am one of these people myself. Yet, quantifying the actual ROI of SCRM can be elusive, and it is dependent on a number of factors:

> ➤ To what degree is your SCRM effectively being utilized?

> ➤ What do you know about your current statistics—those performance areas that you are hoping to improve upon?

> ➤ How will you track your results and what kind of results do you need to consider?

You will need to weigh your investment of time and money against these results, and in many cases, you have to look at activities rather than at the SCRM itself. Social activities are no different than traditional activities. When you ask the question, "What kind of sales ROI are we receiving from social networking?", this should be answered and evaluated in exactly the same manner that we would with any other prospecting method (looking at a sales model). For example, what is the ROI of a cold call? An e-mail? A phone call? A personal visit?

Therefore, we are not calculating the ROI of your Social CRM, per se. *This is important. We are calculating ROI based upon the impacts being realized as the result of specific activities. SCRM merely lets us manage these activities.*

In some cases, you will need to look at more subjective valuations such as, "What is the effective ROI if we have better information about 'x'?" In other words, assuming that you do see a measurable value in having strong customer relationships (you do, don't you?), you will also recognize that these relationships will always lead to increased revenues. Each and every one of following questions points to exactly the same result—a positive effect on your bottom line!

> ➤ Is there value in our people knowing more about our customers and prospects?

> ➤ Does having this information lead to better customer relationships?

> ➤ Do better customer relationships result in increased sales and referrals?

> ➤ How does a strong customer relationship affect customer retention?

> ➤ How does being able to track the effectiveness of social media campaigns affect our bottom line?

> ➤ Do social communities increase brand ambassadors and advocacy?

> ➤ Are our social activities uncovering new leads that are turning into opportunities?

> ➤ By providing social customer service, are we providing better service?

While these questions may be subjective, do not minimize their value! Each addresses a real profit area that can be found in your small business and each affects your return on investment!

Establishing benchmarks

We can also take a look at hard data, such as sales performance or website visits generated by a specific campaign. We will have numbers that we can track and then compare to previous results. In order to make these comparisons, we need to first establish benchmarks that are reflective of our most recent results. I would base these on average figures (values) over your previous 12 months. Once your system is up and running, it should be able to calculate these benchmarks for your based on system history.

These benchmarks may be by individual, by team, by department, by company, or how about for all four? This will take some work! However, if monitoring your increases and evaluating your ROI are important to you, it's worth it. There can be no basis for determination if there is no basis for comparison.

Performance metrics

Once we have established benchmarks for comparison, some of the metrics (numerical values) that you might wish to evaluate and compare include the following:

> **Revenues**: Naturally, we would want to see these go up!

> **New businesses revenues**: New business is one of the most important life-bloods of any business!

> **Revenues from existing customers**: Your existing customers are often an untapped new revenue resource!

> **Referrals and referral sources**: Maximizing your referrals and your referral sources will always lead to increased revenues!

> **Leads and lead sources**: You need to be able to evaluate how your money is being spent on lead generation, what the results are, and where they are coming from.

> **New opportunities**: Opportunities are a metric that can be used to gauge lead generation as well as lead conversion (to a sale!).

> **Total pipeline/forecast**: If there is nothing in your forecast, the chances of hitting your numbers are very slim! The amount of time that each opportunity spends at each stage is another good indicator. Why are some moving forward while others seem to be stuck?

> **Closing ratios**: You always want to increase your closing ratios! If these are going down instead of up, you have adjustments that must be made in your pricing, your offering, your salespeople, or all three.

> **Campaign results**: Campaigns that produce quality leads will produce sales. Those that are ineffective will do neither!

> **Support cases**: There are many metrics surrounding support including number of cases, case types, and time needed for case resolution. All of these should be monitored for increased effectiveness!

> ➤ **Customer retention**: Everybody will lose customers from time to time. In some cases, such as death, you can't do anything about that! In most cases, you can take the steps to save and secure customers and your retention rate must increase consistently.

> ➤ **Cost savings through better utilization of resources**: Sometimes, you need to spend money in order to make money; sometimes, by making better use of your resources, you are accomplishing the same thing. Track and analyze these trends!

Social metrics

Social metrics can also be expressed and evaluated based on hard data, and this should be done for individuals as well as for the company. As before, you will need to first establish benchmarks in order to determine increased effectiveness. Some examples of social metrics include the following:

> ➤ The number of followers or connections you have

> ➤ The number of retweets on Twitter and what is being retweeted

> ➤ How often each update is being shared and on which networks

> ➤ How many people like your Facebook page

> ➤ What social networks are driving people to your website and landing pages

You should ask individuals to provide you with this information as you will not have access to their personal social accounts (nor should you), and asking for things like usernames and passwords is extremely frowned upon. Evaluate each of these networks based on your individual team members' responsibilities. For example:

> ➤ Salespeople will be judged on sales, whereas support personnel may be judged on their ability to handle cases, while marketing might be judged on campaign effectiveness.

> ➤ Salespeople might be evaluated on group activity, support on maintenance of the company's web-based service options, and marketing on effective community management and engagement.

> ➤ All departments should be analyzed to ensure that their messaging is consistent and aligned with your company's goals and standards.

This data can be gathered from individual social networks or through the specific deployment of third-party social tools, many of which were identified in our previous chapter. *Properly focused social activities will result in increased revenues.* The following lists are by no means all-inclusive of the data that is either available to you or that you may wish to gather and evaluate based on your specific small-business needs and goals.

A portion of these lists reflect a checklist of tasks that should have been addressed previously during your initial network setups while the remaining are reflective of numbers that you should be tracking for comparison.

LinkedIn, Facebook, and Google+

As these three networks share a number of common features, we will consider them together. It is critical for your team members and for your company to present a unified presence on all of the social networks. As a team, everyone pulls together in reaching the company's common goals, and this collective energy enables us to leverage our connected strength. This is achieved through our standardized messaging, our image, and our engagement activity.

> ➤ How do their profiles look? Are they complete and configured for search?
> ➤ How many social connections does each have and on each network?
> ➤ Who are they connecting to? Is it reflective of your target market?
> ➤ Are team members connected on these networks?
> ➤ Do employees correctly list your business as their place of work?
> ➤ How often is their profile being viewed?
> ➤ How are people finding their profiles?
> ➤ Are they posting (sharing) updates and how are those being read and shared?
> ➤ What types of updates are being shared? Do they point back to your business?
> ➤ Are they engaging with others?
> ➤ How many, and what groups, do they belong to?
> ➤ Are they engaging in groups?
> ➤ How do your company pages look?
> ➤ Are updates being posted to company pages?
> ➤ How many people are following/liking the company pages on each network?
> ➤ Are new leads and opportunities being discovered as a part of your social networking activities on these networks? Quantities, values, quality?

Twitter

In my opinion, and regardless of the nature of your small business, Twitter can be an invaluable tool for discovering new opportunities (influencers and products/services) and is also a great place to start a conversation that will lead to more meaningful engagements, formal connections, and relationships. Therefore, in order to effectively evaluate system performance, it is important that you track certain metrics.

> ➤ How many followers does each of your team members have, and how many do they presently follow?
> ➤ How many retweets, favorites, and replies are being generated by their followers? These will demonstrate how your messaging is resonating.
> ➤ Are they on any lists and, if so, which ones?
> ➤ What are they tweeting? Is it on target per your company messaging guidelines?

> ➤ Are they engaging with their followers?
> ➤ Are new leads and opportunities being discovered as a part of Twitter activity?

Analytics

Analytic services can go a very long way toward providing you with the social data that you require. For example, Google Analytics (one of many such programs) will include data on website page visits as well as where those page views are originating from (including your social networks).

Many networks, including LinkedIn, Facebook, Twitter, and Google+ (as a part of Google Analytics) will offer either free or paid analytic services that will help you to better understand what activity is occurring within your accounts and pages.

Sharing tools like Hootsuite, Buffer, and bit.ly (among others) can also provide you with analytic reports that may include, for example, how many times any individual update was retweeted to someone's own community. Suffice to say, there are many, many tools that will assist you in these tasks!

Analyzing the results

While hard data results are a good indicator, you must look at the process (how things are being done and whether they are being done correctly) in order to fully understand any indicator, good or bad. This is not a foot race! It will take time, patience, and continual evaluation and adjustment in order to achieve your desired optimal results. Few things in life are perfect *out of the box*. That does not mean that we will not be receiving quantifiable benefits as we perfect our processes. Please do not lose sight of this fact!

In conclusion

As this is our last section, I wanted to take this opportunity to personally thank you for taking the time to read this book (and for spending your hard-earned money on it!). It is my sincere hope that you will find it to be of value in your quest to implement Social CRM in your business. I have no doubt that, if you follow the principles and guidelines that we have outlined for you, you will be successful and you will reap the associated benefits!

We mentioned a number of tools and platforms during the course of this book, and you can find links to each in the next section. Finally, if you have any further questions, reach out to me on LinkedIn!

> Links

A full listing of these links, in a live format, can be found at `http://adaptive-business.com/small-social-book-links/` where you will also find a link to download the needs assessment template that was discussed in *Chapter 4, Define Your Social CRM Needs Prior to Any Investment*.

For your convenience, we have created a list of links that will take you to tools that we have discussed, articles that we have cited, and some excellent recommended resources for your continued reading. Education in the social sphere is never ending and never stops!

Alphabetical list of applications

The following is a list of specific applications and tools that were mentioned in the book:

- **Act-On**: `http://bit.ly/1gzjJgs`
- **Asana**: `http://bit.ly/1c4g79d`
- **AWeber**: `http://bit.ly/1fmCUHM`
- **Bitly**: `http://bit.ly/1et0S41`
- **Box**: `http://bit.ly/1jwQiyb`
- **Buffer**: `http://bit.ly/1hOwWHn`
- **Cazoomi SyncApps**: `http://bit.ly/1nY1i6L`
- **Chrome Webstore**: `http://bit.ly/1mEU5hJ`
- **Constant Contact**: `http://bit.ly/1fQhJ1L`
- **Data.com**: `http://bit.ly/1htG3ZJ`
- **Desk.com**: `http://bit.ly/1jwQRrX`
- **Dropbox**: `http://bit.ly/1htGjb3`
- **edocr**: `http://bit.ly/1bIIHws`
- **Facebook**: `http://on.fb.me/MYdg66`
- **G2 Crowd**: `http://bit.ly/1rPi0dC`
- **Get Satisfaction**: `http://bit.ly/1liIenU`
- **GetApp**: `http://bit.ly/1liIoeX`

- **Google Alerts**: http://bit.ly/1fBMURO
- **Google Analytics**: http://bit.ly/1cjyXnm
- **Google Apps**: http://bit.ly/1bIJCwE
- **Google Drive**: http://bit.ly/1dtPy8i
- **Google News** - http://bit.ly/1cjzzcG
- **Google Voice**: http://bit.ly/1poxG7g
- **Google+**: http://bit.ly/1dtQ5XJ
- **GoToMeeting**: http://bit.ly/MYfxOM
- **Hootsuite**: http://bit.ly/1mEZ8hW
- **Hubspot**: http://bit.ly/1k72OY8
- **iCloud**: http://bit.ly/1hlsfBJ
- **IFTTT**: http://ift.tt/1htK6VM
- **Import2**: http://bit.ly/1efcZpZ
- **Infusionsoft**: http://bit.ly/MYgZAw
- **InsideView**: http://bit.ly/1fBQdZp
- **itDuzzit**: http://bit.ly/1c4kYXT
- **KiteDesk**: http://bit.ly/1gznK4x
- **Klout**: http://bit.ly/1bILDcd
- **Kred**: http://bit.ly/MYhT02
- **Leadfindr**: http://bit.ly/1cjBKg4
- **LeadSift**: http://bit.ly/1hlteBO
- **LinkedIn**: http://linkd.in/1efewMK
- **Little Bird**: http://bit.ly/1c4lOE7
- **MailChimp**: http://bit.ly/1htN6l9
- **MarketMeSuite**: http://bit.ly/MYjGSS
- **Marketo**: http://bit.ly/1fBTfwK
- **Nimble**: http://bit.ly/1esYcU1
- **OFunnel**: http://bit.ly/1gzp4V0
- **Oktopost**: http://bit.ly/1Ac66ze
- **PeerIndex**: http://bit.ly/1fQo8Kn
- **PieSync**: http://bit.ly/1lkKqdz
- **Pinterest**: http://bit.ly/1mvF2mQ
- **Pipedrive**: http://bit.ly/1hOF2Qe
- **Podio**: http://bit.ly/1jwXfzg
- **Quote Roller**: http://bit.ly/1k75iWv

- **RebelMouse**: http://rbl.ms/1rdLjp1
- **SalesLoft**: http://bit.ly/1hlwMnt
- **SkyDrive (now OneDrive)**: http://bit.ly/1fBWCnx
- **Skype**: http://bit.ly/1k9EeTf
- **Socedo**: http://bit.ly/0yfv0X
- **SocialBro**: http://bit.ly/NumyXn
- **Sprout Social**: http://bit.ly/1cLqPiL
- **TimeTrade**: http://bit.ly/1liSv3l
- **ToutApp**: http://bit.ly/1sZ497j
- **Twitter**: http://bit.ly/1et0emZ
- **TweetDeck**: http://bit.ly/1hM09mX
- **Twtrland**: http://bit.ly/1c4rUV7
- **UserVoice**: http://bit.ly/1hOJu1s
- **WebEx**: http://bit.ly/1o3fBbp
- **Wufoo**: http://bit.ly/1cLsLI0
- **YouTube**: http://bit.ly/1du4y5R
- **Zapier**: http://bit.ly/1haGnhq
- **Zendesk**: http://bit.ly/1haGyJQ

Social add-ons for e-mail

Many people will spend a great deal of their working day within their e-mail interface. They may even spend more time here than they will in their actual SCRM. Fortunately, there are some great tools that you can use to bring your social networking (at least on some level) directly into your e-mail. Please check out these great tools!

For Outlook

Please be aware that the suitability of these tools may, to a certain extent, be based on your particular version of Outlook, whether it is web- or desktop-based, and if you are running a Windows or Mac-based system.

- **LinkedIn Outlook Social Connector**: http://linkd.in/1fQozV0
- **Microsoft Social Connector**: http://bit.ly/1htODra
- **Xobni**: http://bit.ly/1o3cHDs

For Gmail and others

Rapportive (owned by LinkedIn) is a really great social add-on for Gmail and some other e-mail systems. **BrandMyMail** and **WiseStamp** can be used to create beautiful custom e-mail signatures that will display links to your social profiles as well as many other features!

> ➤ **BrandMyMail**: `http://bit.ly/1k9Ju9o`
>
> ➤ **Rapportive**: `http://bit.ly/1poMzpV`
>
> ➤ **WiseStamp**: `http://bit.ly/1k772Pp`

Cited articles

The following is a complete list of articles that were cited in the book:

> ➤ **IBM Reveals Their Predictions About The Future Of Social CRM**: `http://bit.ly/qnQDYD`
>
> ➤ **2014 CMO's Guideline to the Social Media Landscape**: `http://cmo.cm/1qNj2Z9`
>
> ➤ **Instructions for converting text to columns**: `http://bit.ly/1bxczVJ`
>
> ➤ **Salesforce "Getting Started Implementation Guide"**: `http://bit.ly/19zxVCh`
>
> ➤ **Social CRM—New Rules of Engagement—Uses by Department**: `http://slidesha.re/1cLoPa6`
>
> ➤ **Social Media's Impact on Customer Service**: `http://bit.ly/1hDB61W`
>
> ➤ **The Ultimate Cheat Sheet for Mastering LinkedIn**: `http://bit.ly/1jCxkUi`

Suggested reading

If you wish to keep up with the latest developments in SCRM, CRM, Sales, Marketing, and Customer Support, these sites provide consistently excellent explorations of these topics. I also suggest that the best way to stay on top of all the latest news from any site that you choose to follow is with an online reader and I would recommend the following sites:

> ➤ **Feedly (recommended reader)**: `http://bit.ly/Nutkwl`
>
> ➤ **Adaptive Business Services**: `http://bit.ly/1et2qLj`
>
> ➤ **CRM Idol**: `http://bit.ly/OyqAix`
>
> ➤ **HubSpot free marketing resources**: `http://bit.ly/1hatAf7`
>
> ➤ **InsideView Blog**: `http://bit.ly/MrddPk`
>
> ➤ **LinkedIn Learning Center**: `http://linkd.in/1fC3dye`
>
> ➤ **Mashable**: `http://on.mash.to/Oymsiz`

- **Maximize Social Business**: http://bit.ly/1cLwuFB
- **Midsize Insider**: http://bit.ly/1cjJX3T
- **Partners in EXCELLENCE Blog**: http://bit.ly/1o3kjFP
- **RazorSocial**: http://bit.ly/0ymPdb
- **ReadWrite**: http://bit.ly/0yn6wK
- **Sales Benchmark Index**: http://bit.ly/1k9Og6Q
- **Sales for Life**: http://bit.ly/1haLjmD
- **Social Media Examiner**: http://bit.ly/MYuMqL
- **Social Media Today**: http://bit.ly/1htZ5iz
- **The Next Web**: http://tnw.co/1liWUmV
- **Social CRM—The Conversation—ZDNet**: http://zd.net/1jx4V4G

www.ingramcontent.com/pod-product-compliance
Lightning Source LLC
LaVergne TN
LVHW081343050326
832903LV00024B/1293